# Become Closer

William L. Montgomery

# Become Closer

## A New Approach
## To Talking
## With
## Those You Love

William L. Montgomery, MA-MFT
Individual, Couples, & Family Therapist

# Become Closer

Copyright 2009 by William L. Montgomery, PhD and MS-Systems Theory, MA-Marriage and Family Therapy, Certified Gestalt Therapist, working with individuals, couples, and families in Doylestown, PA.

All rights reserved. Short portions of text from this book may be reproduced or transmitted provided credit is given and the author is advised. A reviewer may quote passages which may be printed or included in an online review. The illustrations are also copyright 2009 by the author as part of this book.

For information contact the author in Doylestown, PA.
Phone 215-489-0826

Illustrated by Bonnie Long, Princeton, NJ.

Edited by Tahlia Day, Katharos Editing/Proofreading, near Madison, Wisconsin.
www.katharosediting.com

Cover design consultation and pre-publication layout by Elaine Paxson, Big World Design, Furlong, PA.
www.bigwd.com

ISBN 978-0-9641124-5-2

# Note From The Author

The three stools discussed throughout this book are in my office in Doylestown, PA. Each is a handmade rough but sturdy wooden sitting stool.

*Each stool represents a key principle* that facilitates two people in having an effective dialogue without anger and mistrust. The method has come to be simply called the "Three Stools" approach to communications. The whole purpose is to bring couples and families together; to *Become Closer*.

Welcome to this book... and welcome to this easy approach. I hope you enjoy it and benefit from it, as others have.

All the Best,
Bill Montgomery

In *Hamlet*, the character Polonius prepares his son for travel abroad by saying,
"This above all.
To thine own self be true."
William Shakespeare

While Shakespeare's line may appear obvious or easy to do, it is in fact very difficult, and is the essence of a relationship. Also see Chapter 6, Page 55 for more of this from Shakespeare.

# Acknowledgement

We all stand on the shoulders of others,
learning and growing from essentially everyone in some way.

Our family of origin, friends, teachers, writers, coaches, partners,
spouses, and children all influence who we are, and have
influenced who I am.

I deeply appreciate other therapists for their wisdom and support along the way, especially the following: Dr. Donna Tonrey of LaSalle University and her own practice, who makes time to be creative and inspirational; the always helpful Drs. April Westfall and Thomas Hallam, plus the many other wonderful therapists at Council for Relationships, the oldest Marriage and Family Organization in the country; and the always supportive Marjorie Morgan, along with the other competent and giving fellow therapists at Lenape Valley Foundation, a wonderful model of a community mental health facility.

While the approaches in this book are new and unique, the underlying foundation originated in the proven concepts of many therapists of past decades. I am "standing on the shoulders of many." Today, the broad topic of couples talking and sharing has been enhanced by several writers and therapists, including Robert Scuka of Bethesda, MD and Barry Ginsberg of Doylestown, PA, both of whom have been generous and supportive. Also see Appendix 3.

And I especially appreciate the one person that has been on this journey with me, my wife, Loretta. She is a gift. Thank you.

Thank you all.

# - Contents -

# - Contents -
### Continued

# - Contents -

## Continued

# Can I Change Anything?

Sometimes we know change is needed,

We simply cannot see how,

Even when the change we seek is directly in front of us !

For example ...


In the dark, inside the great whale, Pinocchio asked,

"And how long have you been shut away in here?"

"Two years," replied Geppetto.

"Then, my dear father," said Pinocchio, "we must escape now!"

"You speak well," replied Geppetto, "but I cannot swim."

"You know I am made of wood," replied the puppet. "I am a fine swimmer! Climb onto my shoulders."

"Come," he added, "try it and see!"

"The Adventures of Pinocchio"
by Carlo Collodi, 1883
(Pseudonym of Carlo Lorenzini)

---

The way to freedom was directly in front of Geppetto, but he missed it. This book, *Become Closer*, shows you *how to change* to have better communications. "Try it and see."

*Piglet sidled up to Pooh from behind.*
*"Pooh!" he whispered.*
*"Yes, Piglet?"*
*"Nothing," said Piglet, taking Pooh's paw.*
*"I just wanted to be sure of you."*

A.A. Milne
1882–1956, British author of *Winnie-the-Pooh*, 1926

# A New Beginning

This book has one purpose:

## To Improve Relationships.

The initial improvement may be small, or large, or somewhere in between, but the goal is for you to notice an improvement, as many others have. Hopefully you and a special person in your life will be able to say to each other,

"I *am* sure of you."

The communications approaches in this book are primarily for couples in a committed relationship, but the approaches and skills apply well to other relationships. For example, besides applying to you and your spouse or significant other, the communications approaches here can apply to a family member or a close friend.

Some relationships are mildly strained on occasion, and some need major healing. In either case, the approaches presented here are intended to facilitate a significant difference. If the relationship has been severely harmed, the couple would do best to visit a family therapist. The skills offered here are important for healing strained relationships, and important for relationships to be close and loving.

These ideas are not new. They have been presented by others, with various modifications and flavors, in many books and workshops for decades. The explanations, however, are new. The use of "Three Stools" as a simple means to explain and to experience improved communications has proven effective in my practice. So, I want to share the "Three Stools" approach.

The following paragraph describes the concepts. Upon reading it, you may find improbable the idea that, if you follow the communications approaches, relationship closeness can improve. Nonetheless, the ideas and skills work for couples, families, and close friends. The various reasons relationships improve are discussed later in the book. Here, then, is the description:

To gain closeness with our partner, friend, or family member, each of us must first gain an awareness of *three key driving forces* of our inner-self which are represented by the "Three Stools." After gaining an awareness of each of the three driving forces, the next step is to *express each* to the other person. When we express our inner-selves, and when the other person listens to us and takes in our inner experience, conversations can change completely. *Relationships improve.* Tension decreases. Yelling virtually stops. Feelings of being included and close begin.

The value and meaning of each of the "Three Stools" will be developed as we progress through the chapters.

2

# Why Bother?

Some have asked,

"Why bother to talk this way? If I want him/her to do *this* or to do *that* I need to say, *'Do this or that. Just do it!'* Why should I bother figuring out what is going on with me? I just need to tell my spouse what to do!"

To help answer the question "Why bother?" here are two examples of argumentative, caustic, and hurtful dialogues that can be completely changed by the communication approaches in this book. See if these examples are familiar to you …

*The first example* is James and Judy, a young couple with two small children. He works long stressful hours, while she is constantly concerned about the welfare of the children, about their finances, and about their marriage. She is highly attentive to the children's schooling and to their social interactions through dance, piano, soccer, and more. She is often tired, and feels alone in handling the children. James, like Judy, worries constantly about their finances, but James feels left out of the lives of the children. Both carry anger stemming from feeling unsupported, yet both want to feel close.

In this example, James comes home late and exhausted, hoping that Judy will greet him at the door and dinner will be ready; he has only had coffee all day. Instead, neither Judy nor dinner are anywhere in sight. James is instantly upset.

James says:

> *"I don't get it. I told you when I would be home, but there is no dinner! Plus you put the kids to bed already! That wasn't smart!"*

Judy is tired, she feels unappreciated, she had a rough emotional day with her mother who is ill, and she is looking for a little support from James.

Judy says:

> *"Get your own dinner! You think you are the only one who is tired? And don't you dare wake the kids; it took me an hour to get them to stay in their rooms. They are finally asleep!"*

Emotions are running high with this couple. Both are angry. The evening will probably be stressful and tense. Each will be feeling unsupported and even unloved. The children will likely notice the tension and become tense themselves—not a good thing for the kids!

But remember, when you use the skills in this book, the conversation can, with effort, be completely different. Each person can feel heard, and supported, and loved. The children can witness and experience a household with normal, periodic life difficulties but with parents who can work together.

4

*The second example* is Gerry and Joann, who have a cat that must stay inside or it may run away, a possibility that scares Gerry. Joann is going outside one evening. Suddenly, the cat runs by her side and out the door. Seeing this, Gerry is aghast...

Gerry says:
> *"What do you think you are doing? The cat has to stay inside! When she gets out, she could be dead! I have told you a hundred times, but you don't care."*

Joann replies:
> *"She has been out lots of times. So she got out, so what? I could have been watching. But so what, she'll make it back. Don't be such a worrywart."*

We can imagine how contentious this conversation can become. To Gerry, Joann is not concerned about the cat. He believes *he* is the only one that is concerned. Gerry feels unrecognized and not cared about, even though that may not be true.

In fact, Joann loves and cares for Gerry, and she cares greatly about their cat, but tonight she is worried and anxious over things she has not yet discussed with Gerry. Actually, just the thought of talking with him about these bothersome things causes her to be even more nervous. An argument over the cat is causing them both hurt feelings and great sadness. They both feel alone and angry. They go to separate rooms.

These two examples may seem familiar to you in some ways. They are typical of many arguments. Most importantly, arguments like this do not need to happen. There are skills to learn and to practice.

5

The answer to the earlier question, "Why bother?" is actually quite simple: The "old" way of directing, arguing, bickering, and shutting down seldom works well, especially when you want a close relationship. So, if you or your partner have been feeling bewildered by how to move forward in your relationship, how to feel closer, and why you cannot be understood and arguments keep you apart even though you care for each other, this "Three Stools" approach can make a significant difference. If the current or "old" way of interacting has both of you angry and confused, this "new" way can help. Examples of improved dialogue are in Chapter 10.

The approaches in this book recognize that you and your partner may not be connected and intimate in the way you would like. You may feel angry, hurt, empty, alone, confused, and more. Underlying feelings of anger often hide under the smiles and under the day-to-day discussions of who will do the shopping, who will pick up the kids, or what there is to fix for dinner. Conversations occur, but buried anger stemming from arguments leaves people feeling empty and alone in a marriage or a partnership. The "old" way of arguing or shutting down does not work well for a relationship. The anger remains. The "Three Stools" approach can lead not only to productive solutions to problems, but also to your having a true partner as you travel along life's winding path. The "old" way probably has not worked for you; the "new" way can, and it is here, now, for you to use.

## Who Should Read This?

The primary audience for this short book is adult couples: people in committed relationships. The intention is that *both* people in the relationship read this book, and both practice the approaches discussed here. The concepts are not difficult. If only one person commits to reading and learning and trying, the result will probably be less satisfying, but still an improvement. Marriages and unions are intended to reveal new ways for the two individuals in the relationship to grow emotionally. Communications that supports the relationship is critical to that growth, and such communication is the subject here.

Another possible audience is a family member of yours, such as a mother or father, or an adult sibling. The book is not intended for teenagers, although any teenager who would show an interest certainly deserves the opportunity to learn the concepts here. Adults are the primary audience, simply due to the higher likelihood and capacity of adults to connect with their inner emotions compared to most teenagers. However, a significant point to understand if you have a teenager at home is the following:

> If a parent chooses to learn the "Three Stools" ways of expressing themselves, they will generally discover that their teenager, even if not engaging in an in-depth dialogue, will respond better to these ways than to the angry, frustrated expressions they may normally encounter at home.

Finally, another possible audience is a close friend, presumably one with whom you have more tension and arguing than you would like. In this case, you and your friend would both be reading this book and working to practice and apply the inner-self expression that it recommends.

# What Is Required?

When we buy software for a computer, the side of the box says "System Requirements." Under that heading is a description of the minimum capabilities your computer must have for the new software to work. In this brief section, the requirements needed for this "Three Stools" communications approach are discussed, but unlike the software, there is flexibility here. We are, after all, talking about interactions among people, not machines.

## Willingness

If you and your partner in the relationship are both willing and committed to making a change, the relationship automatically has a positive prognosis for improvement. If one of you is willing to dive in and the other is only willing to wade in, that is still a positive beginning. As the communications approach proceeds, hopefully you will both experience encouragement to be more involved and more willing.

If one of you is willing to learn and to try and the other is simply not, then improvement is possible, but it will be more difficult and probably with less benefit. The purpose of a true relationship is, among other things, to support each other and to grow together.

## Persistence

Once you and yours start this "Three Stools" process, I strongly recommend that you do not stop in the middle. Family physicians advise us that stopping a ten-day course of an antibiotic, for example, can allow the bacteria to return mutant and stronger. If, by analogy, we regard anger and heated arguments as bacteria in a relationship, then we can also regard the "Three Stools" approach as a healing process. Keep going. Do not stop. Of course you will not be perfect in talking with each other, but perfection is not the goal. Healing your wounded relationship is the goal. Read, try, practice, read again, talk, and when necessary, find help.

## Help

Finally, applying the concepts discussed here may require a little guidance from a professional, such as a therapist, psychologist, or counselor. The concepts are relatively easy to understand, but actually applying the concepts can sometimes be unexplainably difficult and therefore a bit disappointing to people, initially. Analogies abound here. I can read or even see how to hit a golf ball, but trying on my own is a different and humbling experience. As a teenager I could see my parents driving a car, but once I was behind the wheel, the dimensions became magnified and the simultaneous tasks surprising. Likewise here, reading may be clear, yet trying may be confusing. Some level of initial disappointment may occur. Do not give up. Keep trying. And remember to ask for professional help if needed. This will be a growing experience.

## Speed Reading

*"I took a speed reading course and read 'War and Peace' in twenty minutes. It involves Russia."*

Woody Allen
Born in 1935, Allen Konigsberg is a three-time Academy Award winner. Born, raised, and lives in New York City.

Tolstoy's *War and Peace* is over 1400 pages. A twenty-minute reading would, indeed, miss nearly everything of meaning. While speed-reading this book may also blur important points, there is a way to reach the core of the "Three Stools" approach without reading every chapter. Those readers seeking to dive into a summary of the whole approach, rather than wading in, can start with Chapter 9. Examples of "old" and "new" dialogue can be found in Chapter 10. If you jump to Chapter 9 and feel confused, as if you are drowning in ideas, please do not quit. Simply go to an earlier chapter; that is, swim backward into shallower water. The ideas here are not complicated; the book is meant to be user-friendly. Do not stop, just back up.

The farther backward you can look, the farther forward you are likely to see.

Winston Churchill

# Chapter 1
# Ouch!

*Sticks and stones are hard on bones*
*Aimed with angry art.*
*Words can sting like*
*anything,*
*But silence breaks the*
*heart.*

*Phyllis McGinley*
1905–1978, American writer of poetry
and children's books. Pulitzer Prize
winner, 1961. This poem is in *The*
*Love Letters of Phyllis McGinley*,
Viking Press, 1954.

## What Are Destructive Arguments Really About?

This chapter describes types, styles, and causes of harmful, hurtful arguments. The approaches discussed in this book to preventing and limiting heated debates and upset feelings will be approaches that prevent and limit the *underlying causes* of the arguments from reaching a critical state in the first place. Understanding the underlying causes is, therefore, important to prevent or limit these heated debates that end in anger, emotional separation, and overall trouble. In other words, before we learn and practice how not to fight and how to be in an intimate, close, caring relationship with a partner—the kind of relationship that you may dream about—*let's first understand the underlying causes of harmful, explosive fights.*

11

Meanwhile, keep in mind...

> Arguments hurt.
> Some arguments are destructive.
> Some are, unfortunately, difficult to
>     forget or forgive.
> Difficult, but not impossible.

## Fighting Styles: Many Styles ... No Victories

Let's begin with types of arguments, as listed below. On this short list, you may find one or more styles or types of arguments that you use or your partner uses during heated debates. These are *not* productive styles of arguing; they are simply styles that we commonly use in a default mode, that is, styles that are automatic for us—styles that often revert back to our childhood or teenhood. In those early years, we perhaps had to find ways to defend ourselves, and these were the styles we developed. These are defensive and even attacking styles. But, of course, they do not promote relationship. We are here reading this book to learn new ways ... ways to leave the childhood and teenhood defenses behind.

> *"I am not arguing with you—I am telling you."*
>
> *James Whistler*
>
> 1834–1903. American-born painter and etcher. Best known for his monochromatic painting titled *Arrangement in Gray and Black: Portrait of the Artist's Mother*, but usually referred to as *Whistler's Mother*. Attended West Point military academy, where he failed a chemistry exam; as he himself said later, "If silicon were a gas, I would have been a general."

12

# Styles of Arguing

*Intellectualize:*
> *"That makes no sense at all. It is not logical." (Or) "I can explain exactly what is going on!"*

*Near Perfection:*
> *"I am right, you are wrong ... and ... everyone knows it but you."*

*Denial:*
> *"I did not say that." (Or) "That did not happen, ever."*

*Rejection:*
> *"I don't care what you think." (Or) "Uh-huh, sure." (While rolling eyes to the ceiling)*

*Exaggerate:*
> *"You never get it right. You can't remember anything and you don't want to." (Or) "You always, always, always say you will be on time and you never mean any of it."*

*Sarcasm:*
> *"Sure, like everything else you do." (Or) "Go ahead, interrupt me, I don't mind."*

*Blame:*
> *"You started it." (Or) "It's your fault. I did nothing!"*

You may be able to think of other categories of fighting back, of continuing the heated debate. Note that in each style above, a power struggle is ensuing. Each person wants to win, or be right. But it cannot happen. During a cyclical, dysfunctional, and heated argument, neither person will say they are wrong and the other is right. Perhaps sometimes this occurs, but rarely. And if one person

13

habitually gives in with the sole purpose of ending the argument and having peace, that in itself is problematic for the relationship and needs to be addressed.

Next, let's look at invalidation, an underlying part of arguing.

## Invalidation: "No!!! You Will Not Put Me Down!!!"

Feeling invalidated is a major cause of high tension for couples. Before discussing that, let's first look at the opposite: namely, feeling *validated*. Dictionary synonyms for "validated" include:

- o Confirmed
- o Authenticated
- o Affirmed
- o Corroborated

Not typically in a dictionary, but important in a relationship with another person, are synonyms such as:

- o Accepted
- o Recognized
- o Appreciated
- o Heard, understood
- o Cared about
- o Supported

Validation by our partner or by others we care about, such as family members and close friends, is important to us all. We need some level of validation from those close to us; otherwise, what is a relationship all about? As discussed in the next chapter, relationship means connection ... recurring connection. Mutual caring, support, understanding, appreciation, and acceptance must be a part of a relationship in the true sense of the word. Further, lack of validation creates hurt and anger, and even fear.

14

Lack of validation and invalidation are often the source of unrecognized emotions, the main one usually being emotional hurt. So, invalidation creates hurt, and hurt in turn creates anger. It is the anger that often shows, and certainly shows during arguments. The anger may be so strong as to break through into retaliatory hurtful and harmful behavior, including verbal and physical fights, and even rage. Interestingly, the sense of being invalidated may or may not have been intended by the other person. Usually, in a committed relationship, it is *not intended*, yet it is felt.

Here, for example, is a dialogue that may be similar to many you have witnessed:

> During a dinner conversation at a restaurant, Alan says to Karen, "Tell me all about your growing up on the farm."
> Karen begins, "Well, I loved it most of the ..."
> "What is this side dish you have?" interrupts Alan, as he reaches with a spoon.

Now let's suppose that Alan has interrupted Karen several times tonight, and she stuffed away each one without saying a word. If she is in touch with her emotions, she very likely felt a twinge of being discounted, diminished, and yes, invalidated. But Alan's interruption was not meant to diminish her. He thought he was being curious; maybe even a protector. "After all," he thought, "she might not like the taste, so I'll taste it first." Imagine his shock if Karen said, "Alan, that is the third time tonight that you cut me off! Stop it. I don't like it!" If Karen's *tone* is not attacking, and if Alan would be able to accept that comment in a constructive way, all is well. But if he becomes offended and defends his actions, and if this leads to an angry, unproductive argument

15

between them, then the unintentional invalidation will have redirected an otherwise fine evening to a rather miserable one.

Clearly we have work to do here in learning a new way of talking with each other: the "Three Stools" way. Here is a way of summarizing this critical point:

> Often anger that shows itself through the various styles of arguing discussed above stems from one or both persons *feeling* or *perceiving some message* that they are invalidated by the other person, *even if that message is never intended.* We must take care to validate, recognize, support, and simply listen to our partners. Listening is often the simplest and best gift we can give.

What more can we know about invalidation? As a start, the dictionary synonyms for "invalidated" include:

- o Abolished
- o Canceled
- o Nullified
- o Repealed
- o Set-aside
- o Rejected
- o Voided
- o Rescinded

These are strong words. When someone believes that they have been "canceled" or "set-aside" or "rejected" by someone they care about, someone they want a meaningful relationship with, feelings of hurt and anger are predictable.

16

Further, invalidation has a link to our styles of fighting above. While the styles may appear different from each other, they have one underlying base, one commonality. Through all these ways of fighting we act to defend ourselves in a valiant attempt to *validate* ourselves. We instinctively rise up to defend ourselves when we sense that we are being invalidated. And the reason we defend is basically simple; invalidation by someone means discounting who we are and what we stand for. It is a discounting of our very Self, our existence. (The capitalized "Self" is used here to represent our very being; the sense we have of being a whole person.)

Instinctively we cannot allow that discounting and invalidation; therefore, we fight back. Much of this defending is not conscious thought; it is more automatic. Further, defense of ourselves often takes on an aggressive stance of *invalidating the other person*. Now a mutual self-sustaining argument occurs. Feeling invalidated leads to feeling hurt and angry; defense begins in order to defend one's being, one's Self; the defense often grows into an aggression that attempts to invalidate the other person; they then respond with invalidation; and the cycle has very quickly begun, grown, and reached high temperatures.

## Invalidation May Start Early

You have seen a child raise up on the playground when a ball is suddenly taken away from him by another child, or when another child pushes to be first in line. As children we gained a stronger sense of our "Self" by standing up, embracing our inner strengths, and displaying defensive behavior. Our behavior served to protect us and/or to increase our confidence; it was "adaptive" behavior. But as adults, defensive or avoidant behavior is often "maladaptive." It does not serve us well. It causes rifts between us and our partners. Hiding in a closet from parents' fights, or acting-out with anger, may have been protective for us as children, but it is maladaptive and not helpful for relationships now. You may have heard adults say that they fought with their spouse and felt childish about it. That is a fair description of what occurs; our instinctive defense behavior was automatic in childhood and may still be automatic.

The first psychologist to recognize childhood adaptive and adulthood maladaptive behavior was apparently Sigmund Freud, when he wrote:

> *"The mechanisms of defense serve the purpose of keeping off dangers, and it is doubtful whether we could do without them during our developmental years. But it is also certain that our defense mechanisms may become dangers themselves. These mechanisms are not relinquished after they have assisted us during our difficult years of development. Thus, these defense mechanisms may bring about more alienation of ourselves from the external world."*

Freud, Sigmund (1923). "The Ego and the Id," Strachey, James. (Translation). The standard edition. 1960. New York: W.W. Norton & Company. Anna Freud, his youngest daughter, later expanded this work greatly.

In addition to Freud's work, various recent studies of schoolchildren have uncovered the tendencies of even preschoolers to use denial, one of the arguing styles above, as a means of protecting their own inner Self. Other, more complex defenses develop in grade school and adolescence. We learn to defend at an early age. Such defense is normal, but becomes problematic when we find a supportive partner who wants to be available for us and wants us to be available for them. We continue to automatically and unconsciously use defense mechanisms rather than becoming vulnerable and open in this new, supportive, non-threatening relationship that our past leads us to mistakenly believe will invalidate us.

## Validation: For You and Your Partner

Referring back to the styles of arguing, we can now understand that each is some form of automatic and probably unconscious defense mechanism that we use to protect and bolster our internal feelings about ourselves. Each offers a style or approach to "winning" by attempting to diminish our partner and, in turn, defend and validate ourselves. Of course, our partner is doing the same; attempting to win and to protect their being, their inner Self. The argument quickly becomes explosive. Underneath the arguing each person often feels hurt, perhaps rejected, and more. The closeness you both want deep inside is masked by negative feelings.

How can all of this hurt, anger, invalidation, and fighting be minimized or even prevented? There is a way—by understanding and utilizing the "Three Stools" approach in appropriate and honest ways. This communications approach allows each person to be completely honest, to be in touch with what they need at the moment, to feel recognized and understood by their partner, and to be supportive and understanding of their partner at the same time.

The chapters that follow will explain each of the "Three Stools" and how to use this communications approach.

When you have to make a choice
and don't make it, that is a choice in
itself.

William James

# Chapter 2
# Relationships

*"Having someone wonder where you are... is a very old human need."*

Margaret Mead
1901–1978, noted anthropologist, raised in Doylestown, PA, first known for her book *Coming of Age in Samoa.*

## What Is a "Relationship"?

The word "relation" derives from an Old French word *"relater"* from the 14th century, meaning "bring back, again, to tell, or to recount, or to restore." This definition reveals the spirit of a relationship, namely to have a recurring connection with another living being. A particular relationship may be strong, trusting, honest, and caring, or it may be just the opposite. We want relationships to be inherently positive, but they may not all be as we wish. Yet we can try. We can make efforts to restore friendships, partnerships, and family connections.

Relationships have a dynamic and constant energy; they are perhaps the most powerful, omnipresent influence in the world. Relationships make the world go around, and they make the journey worthwhile. Relationships give us purpose and meaning. Relationships are always around us and in every way a part of us. Think for a moment of your own relationships, including those with your father, mother, children, sisters, brothers, cousins, nephews, nieces, uncles, aunts, butchers, bakers, barbers, hairdressers ... the list is essentially never-ending. And of course the one primary relationship being addressed in this book is the relationship with your significant other; your partner in life. This is often the most important relationship for our growth as adults.

## Candle Ceremony

Perhaps you have seen a candle ceremony at a wedding, or had your own. The ceremony I mean is when the bride and the groom each hold a candle that is lit. The sanctuary is silent and all eyes are on the two committed people as each simply holds and cherishes their own lit candle for a few short minutes. The couple then moves toward a central candle, approaching from separate sides. Often this separate candle is larger and sturdier, as if to be able to burn longer or brighter, or to carry some larger purpose. Both people simultaneously tilt their candles toward the central candle, which we now realize is the unity candle, or some similar name. They light it together. They now have a well lit, bright, and robust unity candle adding more light into all of the relationships witnessing this union.

Then the strangest thing happens, in my view—they each blow out their own candles. Not always, but in some ceremonies, poof, out go both of the individuals' candles. The unity candle is the only one remaining. The idea is clear and in some ways expected. The message is that the couple will now be as one. That certainly is important; teamwork is a foundation for children to see, for parents to have, for young couples to feel, for relationships to flourish. Unity means growing and working together. It means supporting each other. It means validating your partner while being validated by them. Unity is positive. But there is one subtle and certainly unintentional flaw in the symbolism, I believe.

Blowing out the individual candles can also signify each person giving up who they are for the unity of the family. Unfortunately, that does not result in a strong relationship. In order for a couple to be emotionally strong, each person must have emotional strength. The couple as one cannot have full emotional strength unless each does.

Further, for a person in a relationship to come to understand their partner, they must first understand much of themselves. It is difficult if not impossible to understand and empathize with the fears, anxieties, hopes, dreams, and other complex emotions of your partner if you do not experience your own emotions well. You may not understand fully *why* you have fears, or anxiety, or concerns, or feelings of being overwhelmed, and the like, but if you are *aware* of your own emotions, you can then begin to be aware of your partner's emotions and their inner world. This is a key to committed relationships:

*Be curious about and seek to know the inner world of yourself and of your partner.*

A deep relationship requires knowing your own inner world of emotions, feelings, and thoughts, and knowing the inner world of your partner—not just connecting on the tasks to be done, such as who will take the kids to the soccer game or what needs to be done around the house. These tasks and projects are important, but alone, they do not provide a deep relationship. They provide task-connection, but not person-to-person connection. Gaining this understanding requires talking and sharing, which is often more difficult than one might first imagine. But the outcome is a growth of the individuals and of the union; a growth that can happen only because of commitment.

# The Purpose of a Committed Relationship Is Growth

> *"Don't smother each other. No one can grow in the shade."*
>
> *Leo Buscaglia*
> 1924–1998, professor in the Department of Special Education at the University of Southern California. He authored a number of inspirational books on love, including *The Fall of Freddie the Leaf, Bus 9 to Paradise, Living Loving and Learning, Love* and *My Father.*

Being in a committed relationship presents us with the daily, sometimes hourly, challenge of interacting with another person on every human level: physical, mental, emotional, and spiritual. The challenge lies in being continuously willing to share and to be open to the concerns, hopes, wants, needs, and emotional joys and stressors of the other person and to engage in that willingness without feeling a loss of one's own Self. The challenges are:

- o To engage rather than run.
- o To respond with a willingness to hear and to be heard, rather than react with anger.
- o To consider each tension-filled situation as an opportunity to learn about one's Self and about the other person.
- o To regard each argument as a gift from which to learn; perhaps a gift wrapped in ugly paper, but a gift nonetheless.

Opportunities to learn about ourselves in expansive ways often come through the tensions of a committed relationship. Those tensions may feel daunting and threatening at first, but they can be transformed into feelings of connection and growth; growth of each person and growth of the relationship.

24

# Relationships Build More Relationships

To gain another insight into the significance and impact of the relationship you share with your partner, note that forming a committed partnership means bringing your one special person closer, but it also means inviting new friends—their friends—to be closer to you as well. To visualize this expansion of relationships, imagine a large wheel like a super-large bicycle wheel with you and your partner at the center and the spokes radiating out to your families, friends, and acquaintances. This wheel can include all of the relationships you have at work, at home, everywhere.

The union of the two of you at the center means that your friends and their friends become mixed into this wheel. Before the joining, you had your wheel of family and friends, and your partner had theirs. Now, however, two wheels full of relationships have combined into one larger wheel. This new wheel of family and friends is not only large, it is complex, with more interactions and cross-connections, different levels of emotional connectedness, and different shared interests.

We often do not realize how our close relationship with one person influences our relationship with others. And all of these provide some level of an opportunity to grow. If we can understand our own inner-selves in ways that allow us to connect better with others, we will notice a change in ourselves and in our connectedness with a large circle of people. This little book is intended to facilitate those connections, especially your connection with your partner.

## Arguments Are Close to Home

If you make a list of your relationships, which can be a very long list if you include the mechanic, the baker, teachers, et cetera, you will very likely notice that the list can be divided into two categories of people: those with whom you have no arguments and those with whom you do. Further, you may well notice that those with whom you do have arguments *tend* to be those in your family. This latter point assumes, of course, that you do not have an antisocial neighbor who is creating legal problems or the like. We argue with our family members because, in the simplest terms, our inner psyches inform us that they are the ones who can hurt us emotionally.

> *There's one sad truth in life I've found*
> *While journeying east and west—*
> *The only folks we really wound*
> *Are those we love the best.*
> *We flatter those we scarcely know,*
> *We please the fleeting guest,*
> *And deal full many a thoughtless blow*
> *To those who love us best.*
>
> Ella Wheeler Wilcox
> 1850–1919, American poet known as the people's poet,
> expressing the need for kindness and joy in life. Best known
> for her poem which begins "Laugh and the world laughs
> with you."

To protect ourselves from "those we love the best," we fight back, often in ways that are unproductive and that exacerbate the situation. But we feel a need to defend, to prevent emotional harm, to stand up for who we are. The defense goes back to Chapter 1 on explosive arguments and why they occur: to preserve our sense of "Self."

If you are reading this book because you are in a caring relationship but the arguments seem to have a life of their own, with the result that you and your partner do not feel close, then this concept of arguing "with those we love the best" needs to be explored. In particular, a critical point to explore within your inner

26

psyche is that you may be—perhaps for the first time but you do not know it—in a caring relationship with someone who is there to listen, care, support, and generally validate you to a level that you may never have experienced before. If you are reading this last point with skepticism about your partner's intention to support you, to truly be available to you, and to show their caring for you, that skepticism is fully understandable. If you felt fully supported and loved by your partner, you probably would not have an urgency to read this book. But, through your skepticism, you may also have a hope and a small inner belief in your heart of hearts that your partner really does care … if only they knew how to show it, or if only the anger between the two of you could recede long enough for a new beginning to emerge.

Most often the truth in a seemingly difficult, conflict-filled relationship is that the caring is still present, even if deeply buried beneath the surface, but the couple has few skills to repair the tears, the anger, the hurt feelings, and the mistrust that has grown over time. New skills are needed. Like most new skills, they are fairly easy to explain and to understand, but practicing them takes time and cooperation between two people, which creates a challenge. A significant challenge lies not only with the other person, that is, not in one's partner who "just does not get it," but with each one of us as we attempt to express ourselves. In other words, the challenge is with ourselves as *expressers of our inner selves*, not only with our partners in learning how to listen.

Remember that relationships allow emotional growth, and that looking at your inner Self in new ways for the first time is the beginning of that growth; a growth that will serve you well in your committed relationship and with all of your family and others. The journey may be doubtful for you, and you may look to your partner to do more, but remember to concentrate on your own inner Self ... that is the challenge!

To find fault is easy; to do better may be difficult.

Plutarch
Greek Historian
46 – 120 A.D.

# Chapter 3
# Toothpaste

*"I argue very well. Ask any of
my remaining friends. I can
win an argument on any topic,
against any opponent. People
know this, and
steer clear of me
at parties. Often,
as a sign of their
great respect,
they don't even
invite me."*

Dave Barry
Born 1947, American
writer and humorist
known for his weekly
newspaper column
and his many books.

Arguments are not actually about how to load the dishwasher, or about wrong and right ways to squeeze the toothpaste tube. Couples do, indeed, have heated and nasty arguments over these and similar subjects, but the argument is not about—not driven by—the subject itself. Unfortunately, the couple actually believes at the time that the argument is very much about loading the dishwasher, or squeezing the toothpaste, or picking up the kids, or folding the laundry, but it is not. Chapter 1 discussed underlying feelings of being diminished or invalidated by another person as a relentless motivator for defense and argument. We have, then, two levels of an argument: the content or subject matter level of the argument, and the emotional level. The toothpaste level and the emotional-Self level.

Building on this idea of two levels in an argument, this chapter describes a two-step or two-level model that helps explain how and why people are unable to release themselves from a heated verbal confrontation. The two-step model is intended as an aid in understanding how to have disagreements without the anger, hurt, and feeling of a wedge between you and the other person.

## The Two-Step Ladder

As you can no doubt discern by now, heated and raging arguments are not usually about the subject that appears to be the center of the argument. Instead, the battle is actually over each person's struggle to prevent feeling discounted by the other person. A graphic way of seeing this is to imagine an old-fashioned wooden ladder with rungs as steps between two wooden sides.

This particular ladder has only two rungs; two round horizontal bars. The top rung represents the content of the argument; the subject of the discussion. It could be a trash can that is not being taken to the curb when your partner wants, or a phone call home that you did not make while your partner sat at home worrying, or a child who one of you thinks needs to be in bed asleep and the other does not. These are all examples of top-rung content items. The top rung contains the tasks, "to-do" items, facts, opinions, and situations that happen. In general, we can say that the top rung contains "things." The second or bottom rung is the location of the "Self." On this level is our inner Self, which we are placing into this conversation and which we want to be heard and

appreciated. This is the same idea of Self first discussed in Chapter 1 on page 17.

I believe that virtually every time we have a conversation with our partner, we are communicating on both levels, both rungs. The difficulty is that we are often unaware of how to handle a two-level conversation, especially when it becomes a heated, contentious argument.

Let's explore the levels of conversations further. To the arguing couple, the heated and hurtful fights appear to be about the content-oriented top-rung items: the facts, the tasks, etc. Further, the fighting styles discussed earlier keep the argument on the top rung. For example, one person will deny what the other says is fact, or will reject, refute, or blame the other for doing something wrong. All of this takes place on the top rung. On this top rung the argument may start small, then suddenly grow, leading to an explosion like a volcano, with each person attacking, blaming, denying, rejecting, etc. For example:

*Judy, explosively angry and pointing at Bob:*
"You said *you* would pick up the girls; don't pretend you didn't!"

*Bob, teeth clenched:*
"Not true! I *asked* if you wanted me to, I *never* said I would. Don't *tell* me what I said."

*Judy, eyes glaring:*
"They are stuck at school because of *you*. You are completely and always unreliable!"

The argument continues … about who is right, and who is wrong.

I call this a "Level 1" conversation or argument. It is on top, on the surface. It is about the content, but is not about the real underlying issues. It may appear that the issue is that Bob is not reliable, or that the girls are stuck at school, or that Judy contorted Bob's original answer. In truth, none of these choices describe the underlying substance of the conversation they are having. Something else—that second rung, or the "Level 2"—is emotionally holding them in a deadlock argument.

Judy and Bob do not know it yet, but they are stuck in an arm-waving animation on the top rung of this two-step ladder, with no clue at this point about what is fueling the deep flames of this argument. As a result, each feels unheard, each is becoming visibly torrid with anger, and each will perhaps become emotionally disconnected and shut down. They need a way to both identify the underlying issues and have the courage to discuss them.

## Memory: One Week Later

Next week this couple, who had a super blow-out Level 1 argument, will likely remember that they had a horrific argument, and they will remember that it felt awful, and they will still carry some of the anger, but they may *not remember* what the argument was about! This lack of detail while retaining the emotions is common. The couple will have some mixed memory of how they each felt, which is the lower rung of the conversation ladder, but they probably will not remember the content of the argument; the upper rung. They forget the details ... but retain the emotions.

There is a meaningful message in the fact that the emotional memory is retained but the detailed memory is faded. That message, I believe, is that one's *emotions* are the important component of the discussion. In other words, the real issues lie at the bottom rung of this two-level ladder. This is Level 2 where one's emotional Self resides. While every argument concerns some top-rung Level 1 facts about who placed the car keys where, or about what one heard the other mumble while going past them in the kitchen, the real depth of the conversation lies on the lower rung, on Level 2. The real issue for this couple, and for all of us, likely has something to do with feeling appreciated, or heard and understood, or cared about—this is Level 2.

## Too Tight a Connection

The two-step ladder analogy is not only relevant because two levels exist in a conversation and we need to learn to talk to each other on both levels, but also, and critical to the conversation skills process, the two levels are connected. This connection is a principal underlying cause of the heated debates that occur.

The concept of the two levels being tied together can be seen, in one way, from the perspective of childhood development. As children we come to view objects that we have attachment to as reflecting ourselves. A child's artwork on the wall reflects something about them; they may, for example, be proud of their skill and therefore of themselves. A child's skill at soccer can, in part, represent who they are, their inner Self. A child taking another child's ball at age four or five likely results in the Self of that second child being challenged, as if they personally have been diminished by the ball being taken.

These examples are intended to demonstrate that the two levels of Content and Self are connected in our childhood and that connection influences our *unconscious tie* between the two as adults. Further, that unconscious tie automatically stimulates us to react to any of the fighting and attacking modes of denial, rejection, blame, et cetera, with defense of our inner Self. We hear or perceive a rejection at Level 1 concerning some fact, object, or opinion to which we are attached, and we rise not only to defend our content position, but to defend our Self. For us, the two are unconsciously tied together.

The difficulty arises in how we explain our positions. When we do this poorly, even though we are in a committed relationship in which we support and care for each other, feelings of being diminished or ignored can overpower the feelings of being loved and accepted, and a horrific argument can begin. One objective of this book is to provide guidance in *emotionally separating* the two levels: the Content and the Self. When this separation occurs, a person can know that their idea may be rejected by their partner, but their Self remains fully accepted. Their view of a situation can be judged as skewed, but they are fully accepted for who they are without condition. The separation is key to preventing a relationship wedge. Both levels of the two-step conversation ladder must be discussed but decoupled.

We have all heard the phrase "Don't take it personally" as a suggestion on how not to become angry or upset at a situation, probably one that we do in fact take personally. That phrase is calling for a separation between the two levels of our conversation ladder. A significant concept here is that for the best possible growing relationship, the two levels, or the two rungs of this ladder, need to be separated. We as partners in a relationship need to own our opinions and emotions while accepting that the other person also has opinions and emotions that they own.

The challenge becomes this:
> In a caring relationship, when our ideas are not readily accepted by "those we love the best," we need to internalize and remind ourselves of the following points:

o Our ideas, opinions, judgments, and viewpoints can be unacceptable to our partner, but *we* ourselves are accepted and cared about.

o Our opinions can be called invalid, but *we* can feel fully validated. Sometimes we need to validate ourselves, rather than looking for validation from outside.

o Our viewpoints can be thought strange or out of place, but *we* are cared for and truly loved.

In summary, another value of the "Three Stools" approach lies in its capacity to facilitate a separation between Content and Self, and to facilitate validation of one's partner while validating one's own Self. This approach can become a natural pathway, a natural way for you and your partner to interact.

There is nothing permanent
except change.

Heraclitus
Greek Philosopher
535-475 B.C.

# Chapter 4
# You

*"You grow up the day you have your first real laugh, at yourself."*

**Ethel Barrymore** 1879–1959, Academy Award-winning actress, born in Philadelphia, proposed to by Winston Churchill, and great-aunt of actress Drew Barrymore.

The last three chapters discussed:

- o The nature of arguments, especially destructive arguments.
- o The nature and importance of relationships, which our lives depend upon.
- o A "two-step ladder" model describing how we become locked into and confused by arguments.

The objective of this chapter is to provide an understanding of the elements or dimensions of human nature and wellness in order to thereby understand ways in which we can improve who we are and how we interact. Further, this chapter is in preparation for Chapters 5 and 6, which describe the "Three Stools" for communications, and for Chapter 7, which explores our own barriers to implementing the improved communications approach. In other words, this chapter and the previous chapters are an important foundation for the chapters on communications and improving closeness that follow. This foundation is important because it offers a helpful way of understanding "You as a Whole Person," and can thereby provide a basis for improved connection with those you love. All of this will become clearer as points are discussed and examples are given.

## You; The Whole Person

The Whole Person Model, which is based on an ancient oriental philosophy, suggests that human beings are comprised of four elements or dimensions:

o *Physical*, which includes every aspect of our physical selves, from facial expressions, to hunger, sexual drive, and thirst, to exercising for health, and all of our five senses. This dimension is best represented by a picture of a whole body.

o *Mental*, which includes learning, thinking, knowledge, opinions, understanding of facts, planning, analysis, and memory. These occur primarily in the brain learning and memory areas; see Appendix 1. This dimension could be represented by a picture of a person reading a book.

o *Emotional*, which includes any and all feelings and emotions that we experience throughout the day, from joy to sadness, from relief to stress, and from loneliness to feeling overwhelmed. Emotions are known to originate in special areas of the brain, but they can often be felt in physical ways. Emotions often show in our body language, especially in our eyes and face.

38

o   *Spiritual,* which is experienced in different ways by different people, but can include a sense of connection and belief in a higher power, a universal consciousness, or oneness with nature or mankind. This dimension can probably not be represented easily. The personal nature of spirituality certainly depends upon our mental and emotional states, and for some can be felt physically.

The Whole Person Model is the same concept referred to in medical circles when practitioners address "treating the whole person." This model delineates the four dimensions—the four realms of us—that we can explore, expand, and exercise in order to grow as individuals and in our relationships.

Further, we can recognize from this model that *relationship* growth (which is different from physical or body growth) requires *emotional* growth, perhaps followed by some beneficial growth intellectually and spiritually, depending upon the couple and their interests. A couple saying "We want to grow together" is shorthand for "We want to grow emotionally, intellectually, and spiritually together," yet couples rarely realize or identify those three dimensions that are actually involved in the growth.

Each dimension of the Whole Person Model will challenge us over time, and each will change over time. We have different views, opinions,

39

understandings, emotions, responses, interests, and of course physical attributes in our 20s than we do in our 30s, 40s, et cetera. *We change because each dimension of our Whole Person changes.* Our lifetime work—hopefully enjoyable and interesting work—is to guide those changes as best we can with the goal of improving who we are, for ourselves and for our relationships with our partners, family members, children, and friends.

The next section discusses growth for each dimension of the Whole Person Model.

## Growing Each Dimension

### Physical Growth

Physical growth and maintenance is perhaps the easiest dimension. It simply happens from childhood forward. But as we all know, guiding that growth in healthy ways through healthy eating, regular exercising, curbing harmful habits, and sleeping well is not so easy. Healthy and guided growth requires effort and perhaps discipline. However, for some people, physical growth is still significantly easier than the next level: mental improvement.

### Mental Growth

Our mental dimension encompasses all of our cognitive processes: all the thinking we do. Growth here begins in toddlerhood, and continues into adulthood. Learning the three Rs (reading, writing, 'rithmetic), studying and learning in school, problem solving, learning about the solar system, reading the newspaper, and trying to understand how our electoral process works are all examples of mental growth. Some people have little interest in intellectual pursuit, while others relish mental acuity. The former may have difficulties in school or college, simply because mental growth is required and they do not have the interest, while the latter group is attracted to school and learning.

As we will see later, this mental part of us is, and has been, key to developments and changes in the world, yet it is also the generator of opinions and directives that can trigger those horrendous and heated arguments that you and your partner or family member would like to end. Further, you may already notice that being motivated to learn and being unmotivated to learn are both emotionally driven states. A person can be driven to learn by *fear* of failure without an education, or by *hope* for a better future, or by a *passion* for knowledge. Likewise, a person can be unmotivated to learn for a variety of emotional reasons.

So here we have our first clue that these parts of us in the Whole Person Model are very much interconnected: Mental growth requires learning while emotion provides the drive and the desire to learn. And, at this point in the discussion of the model, we may begin to wonder how much of our behavior ... of everything we do ... is driven by our emotions.

## Emotional Growth

Emotions are, I believe, the central force of our being and of our relationships. Neurologists have found that several areas located in the center of the brain, just above the brain stem, create, facilitate, and support emotions, including behavior and memory associated with emotions. The emotion-related brain areas include names you may have heard before, such as the hippocampus, hypothalamus, amygdala, and prefrontal cortex. These areas work together as one system, called the limbic system, to establish both our feelings and our behavioral responses, such as an increased heart rate, a smile, an urge to run, or an overall feeling of euphoria.

Through this limbic system of our brain, there is both an automatic and memory-based response to situations, events, words, and thoughts that in turn generate our emotions. These interconnected areas of our nervous system generate all of the single-word descriptors of emotions that you can conjure up: happy, sad, depressed, rejected, hurt, afraid, blamed, attacked, and so many more.

Emotions are often in the driver's seat of our lives, and changing directions can be difficult. It can be done; emotions of trust, closeness, and joy can increase and relationships can improve, but conscious and deliberate effort is required. Growing and improving emotional health are difficult for most people. Emotions can be triggered easily, but changing one's emotional reaction to a trigger or the level of the reaction is often difficult.

If we want to improve physically, we exercise or eat well, both of which are direct pathways or inputs to the physical self. Likewise, if we want to improve our mental acuity and knowledge, we can read, study, or take a course. The pathway into the mental is direct. But if we want to grow, improve, explore, or expand emotionally, the purposeful-growth pathway is less direct into the emotional brain center, the limbic system. Other parts of the brain—the thinking, hearing, seeing, touching, analyzing, fact-seeking, problem-solving, and understanding parts—become involved first. Generally, the result is that a deliberate, conscious effort is required to improve our emotional health.

Talk therapy is an effective pathway to emotional growth, even though it is an indirect path into emotional brain centers. The discussion must be processed through the intellectual or mental parts of us, then be internalized in such a way as to be effective in reducing depression, sadness, self-doubt, anxiety, et cetera. The most common pathway into our emotions that allows growth is through our mental realm. For some people, the spiritual realm also provides a pathway to improved emotional health. Further, we can recognize that psychotropic medications can improve emotions and mood. While they are not a cure-all or a final solution, medications have been vastly important.

## Same Model but a Unique Person

The Whole Person Model applies to all of us, and yet we are all absolutely unique. In the physical dimension, no one in the world looks exactly like anyone else. Not even identical twins are completely identical. This is amazing considering there are over six billion people in the world. We are all physically unique. Further, we are all different mentally, that is, in how we think, and what we think, and what we know, and how we express it. We all have different intellects and different thought processes. And, most importantly, we are different emotionally. Logic suggests that no two people in the world have exactly the same emotional composition or make-up. Depression, for example, is not experienced in the same way by everyone, and while we can likely find two people who would describe their depression in very similar ways, their actual experience might not be precisely the same if it could somehow be measured.

Interestingly, it is impossible to finitely describe these mental or emotional differences because we can not see them or measure them as we can for physical differences. The difference in height between two people, even twins, can be measured to a fraction of an inch. Anyone can measure the space between a person's eyes, or the length of their earlobe, or the length of their philtral dimple (that groove between one's nose and lip), and you can compare your measurements to those of someone else. Measurement is not as simple or as definitive for mental differences or emotional differences, and yet we know the differences are present.

In summary, we are all unique in every dimension: physical, mental, emotional, and spiritual. We all have different personalities and different ways of thinking. We have different opinions, viewpoints, feelings, reactions, wishes, dreams, desires, and goals. All of these are formed, contained, and changed from time to time by that amazing mass of neurons called the brain.

Now let's explore the interactions that occur in our inner selves that actually make us who we are and also explore some interactions that are involved between ourselves and others.

## Thinking Links to Emotions

Expecting the physical, mental, emotional, and spiritual dimensions of us to exist side by side without interacting might be an easy and simple way to model us as people in this world of complexities and relationships, but in fact, the interplay among these four dimensions is strong and often instantaneous and unconscious. We can think that someone hung up the phone on us and instantly become frustrated, hurt, and perhaps angry at them. If we think instead, "The cell phone company did it again, they cut us off," we may still be angry, but not at the other person, and perhaps not with the same intensity. The emotions are different, and are a direct result of what we are thinking. We are not, however, normally aware of this interdependence.

In psychology this link is recognized as potentially helpful for people, if they are able to redirect their thinking in a helpful way. The redirecting process is called "reframing." The result of reframing is a reduction in one's anger or anxiety. If, for example, Joe, a salesman, experiences being cut off in the phone call mentioned above, he can *choose* to allow the possibility that it was the phone company and not the party on the other end of the call. In this way, he reduces his anger, he can remake the call, he can be calmer and more functional, and he can allow himself and the other person to deal with whatever actually happened. Similarly, Vanessa, a computer consultant, can reframe by creating a truth for herself that the sales clerk did not purposely ignore her, or that making a wrong turn while coming home from the city allows her to see a new part of the suburbs, so there is no need to be angry at herself.

So, next time you feel angry, you might ask yourself what you are thinking that might be creating that anger. Likewise, if you feel joy, depression, or anxiety, notice what you are thinking. Our thinking often affects our emotional state.

## Thinking, Emotions, and Behavior

The above two paragraphs contain examples of how our thoughts result in certain emotions. But there is more to explore here. Namely, thoughts can lead to emotions that in turn lead to emotion-driven behavior. If Vanessa makes a wrong turn, then frames it in her mind as "being stupid," she may become angry, and her behavior may show it. She may hit the steering wheel, speed up the car, and panic to find an opportunity for a U-turn. Her behavior will not be pleasant for anyone in the car, including herself. If she reframes to thinking, "This is an opportunity to see something new around here," she can feel calm, not angry, with the behavioral result that she can discuss the possibilities with her passengers calmly. She can laugh, they can all be calmer, and they can all feel more connected. Reframed thinking can improve mood, which can improve behavior. As a side comment, to show the complexity of all of this, note in this example that the *behavior of one person* in the car affects the *emotions of others* in the car, which in turn affects *their behavior.*

## Your Whole Person Interacting with Their Whole Person

We are complex. As discussed, the physical, mental, emotional, and spiritual dimensions, or realms, of ourselves very much inter-relate; they affect each other. Our complexity is increased by the fact that a relationship with another person is the interaction of our elements with theirs. Perhaps we can all begin to understand how difficult relationships can be when we realize that we not only have to attempt to understand ourselves in terms of the thoughts, emotions, and physical feelings that are occurring within us, but in order to grow a relationship in healthy ways, we need to understand something of the other person's inner Self. Clearly, to gain this understanding requires a willingness to share. A willingness for each of us to speak our own inner truth and to listen intently to our partner. Further, we need to understand, or at least be willing to try to understand, the interaction that occurs between *our* inner Self and *their* inner Self. Even the attempt to learn and develop the skills required to be aware means growth is occurring. The process of learning about our interactions, both within ourselves and with our partner, is both simple and complex, frustrating and fun, hopeful and confusing; but it is always growth if we stay with it.

In short, the key to growth of one's Self, and to growth of the relationship, lies in each of us recognizing our own inner world and in expressing that to our partner, who is there to hear and to understand. Note that two aspects are involved, both the expressing by one person and the involved listening of another. These two aspects form the solid basis of a relationship and will be discussed in more detail in later chapters.

46

# Chapter 5
# Naming the Three Stools

*"There are three things extremely hard: steel, a diamond, and to know one's self."*

Benjamin Franklin
1706–1790, one of the
founders of the United
States. Also an author,
printer, politician, scientist,
inventor, and diplomat.

The previous chapter described the four dimensions of every human being and called those four dimensions taken together the "Whole Person Model." The model not only delineated the four dimensions, it suggested that a person is wise to address all four in order to have a sense of wellness and wholeness. Holistic doctors and practitioners use the Whole Person Model to address improving health in patients. Remember the four dimensions or elements of each of us: physical, mental, emotional, and spiritual.

This chapter proposes that there are three prime driving forces of our relationships: two from the Whole Person Model, and one other. The "Three Stools" are named for these three forces: *Thinking*, derived from the mental dimension of the Whole Person Model; *Emotions*, also from the Whole Person Model; and a third driving force called *Wants and Needs*.

The majority of this chapter will describe the Wants and Needs force, since it has not been previously discussed. Further, this chapter only *identifies* the "Three Stools," which represent effective "sitting" and talking areas during a conversation. The next chapter describes how to connect well with others by talking from these three areas.

## Our Mental and Emotional Driving Forces

Across all of our mental capabilities—which include memory, our five senses, speech, and thinking—the latter, in particular *analytical thinking*, is the only mental area assigned here as one of the "Three Stools" communication areas. Details of analytical thinking will be discussed in the next chapter. The point here is that our thoughts are a primary driver affecting our connection to others. The second primary driver is our emotions, and the third is our wants, needs, and wishes, which will be discussed in the next section.

A first reaction of some will be that the physical part of us—in particular, physical attraction or even sexual connection—is the driving force, especially during the early stages of a romance. But the fact is that physical attraction and sexual connection are driven by and supported by our thoughts and our emotions. The fairly well-known phrase, "Our main sex organ is our brain," is exactly the point here.

In a committed relationship women will generally say they want to feel cared about (or cherished, or loved) *before* they want to "make love." The emotional state of feeling cherished stimulates a desire for sexual connection. Men in a committed relationship who begin to connect with their internal emotional selves generally discover that they, too, want to feel loved and cared about (yes, it's true), which for them happens before and especially *during* sharing in sexual contact with their partner. In either case, feelings and thoughts initially drive the physical connection. And, yes, the resultant physical connection in turn causes emotional and mental changes in us. This back-and-forth interplay adds to the complexity and variety of how our minds operate. We are fascinatingly sophisticated.

Stressing the two areas of Thinking and Emotions does not discount the importance of the physical or the spiritual elements of us. It is impossible to be without them. Our physical part allows each of us to be active, to hold our partner's hand, to be intimate, to show frustration on our face, to hug our children and parents, and so much more. Of course it is essential. But in this "Three Stools" approach, the physical ... hugs, facial expressions, eye contact, tone of voice, hand-holding, and much more ... is viewed as the *way* we connect, driven by the Mental-Thinking and Emotional parts of us. Our thoughts and our emotions are the essential beginnings that allow us to first imagine the type of relationship we desire, followed by an emotional drive and a trust that enables connection in the first place. Further, what a person *thinks* can, and most likely will, affect how they *feel* about a situation. On the other hand, emotions can influence cognition. If someone feels *lonely*, they may, and probably will, start *reading* ads and billboards about relationships, a subject that has long been researched and understood. The emphasis here, therefore, is on these two, Thinking and Emotions, as the brain-function starting areas for relationships.

## A Third Driving Force: Wants and Needs

There is a third area—the third stool—that we have not yet discussed. This area is:

o   *Not* one of the four dimensions: Physical, Mental-Thinking, Emotional, Spiritual.
o   *Crucial* to explore when developing or working to improve a relationship.

- o *Created* from the intersection of our cognitive or thinking mind and our emotional mind (Mental + Emotional).
- o *Simple* to describe and comprehend as a concept, yet *difficult* for the great majority of people to initially put into action; practice is required.

Imagine, if you will, that our Mental-Thinking dimension and our Emotional dimension, as tied together as they are, together generate an important driving force in us called "Wants and Needs." The term "Wants and Needs" is really shorthand for ...

Wants, Needs, Goals, Wishes, Likes, and Dislikes.

For relationships to flourish, partners must be able to first understand their own individual "Wants and Needs," and then be able to express those to others.

## Awareness of Our Own Wants and Needs

If you are emotionally saturated, you may *need* some space and time to yourself to be alone. But are you aware enough to ask for it? If an important event is planned for next week, you may *want* or even *need* to set aside time to prepare, but can you ask others to honor that? If you are being confused or stressed by an argument with your significant other, you may not only need a break, but also want and crave closeness with your partner, if only you could figure out how, and if you could express it.

Unless we are practiced at being *aware* of ourselves, we tend not to know clearly what we want or even what we need. We are not in touch with ourselves well. Sometimes, for example, we are angry at our partner for not providing what we would like, when in fact we have not expressed it clearly to ourselves or to them. We often do not know ... really know ... what we want, so we don't express it. Or, as is common, we may not be at all aware that we are not aware of what we want, so, certainly, we do not express it. We may talk around it and think we are being clear, when often we are not clear at all because we have not become clearly aware of our own needs.

## Our Hierarchy of Needs

Psychology pioneers discussed wants and needs in various ways. Abraham Maslow, a groundbreaking humanist, identified adult human needs in a hierarchy. Let's review the Maslow hierarchy and determine the extent to which we are or are not in contact with our needs. The base, or first level of the hierarchy, is Physiological Needs, such as food, shelter, and sleep. At this level, we are readily aware of what we need.

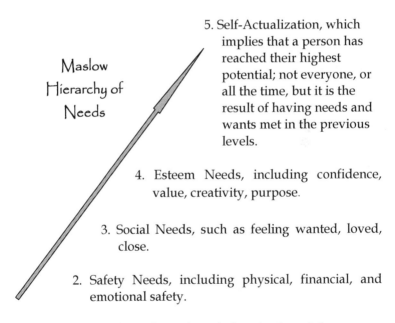

Maslow
Hierarchy of
Needs

5. Self-Actualization, which implies that a person has reached their highest potential; not everyone, or all the time, but it is the result of having needs and wants met in the previous levels.

4. Esteem Needs, including confidence, value, creativity, purpose.

3. Social Needs, such as feeling wanted, loved, close.

2. Safety Needs, including physical, financial, and emotional safety.

1. Physiological Needs, such as shelter, food, and sleep.

The second level of the hierarchy is Safety Needs, such as physical safety, financial security, health, and emotional safety. People are generally aware of their needs at this level. We have all had times when we felt financially insecure or physically unsafe. We are aware of these basic needs.

The third level, Social Needs, covers the need to feel wanted, to be a part of a group or a loving family, to be intimate, to feel loved. While we are keenly aware of needing physical and financial security, as adults we sometimes mentally put aside the need to feel close and cared about, especially if we are carrying anger or are a bit fearful of being close. Yet, being in touch with this need and giving it expression is important. We will talk more about this in the next two chapters.

The fourth level is Esteem Needs, which encompasses the need to feel confident, have the respect and appreciation of others, and have a feeling of achievement toward a purpose. While it may seem obvious that we are all aware of our need for self-esteem, in fact this need can be difficult to delineate and clarify within ourselves. We can be confused when trying to delineate our goal or purpose in life or even within a marriage. We can be fuzzy when attempting to talk about how worthwhile we feel, or about being lovable, or if we can forgive ourselves for past mistakes, all of which relate to self-esteem. The early psychologist Alfred Adler recognized the importance of having and voicing our goals—our wants and needs—as an aid to healing from depression, anxiety, and an "inferiority complex," a term apparently first used by Adler.

Maslow termed the top level of his hierarchy "Self-Actualization," a level that encompasses morality, creativity, open-hearted willingness, low defenses, high desire to learn and improve, low judgmental attitude, and high confidence. In short, says Maslow, at this level a person has reached their fullest potential. Maslow did not expect that everyone could attain this level, or that it was possible to constantly be at this level, but it is a goal in his model. For Maslow, reaching this high level is conditional upon meeting the four types of needs below this level in the hierarchy. Clearly, recognizing our internal wants and needs, being able to express them, sharing them with a partner, and working to achieve them are important aspects of our growth and the growth of our relationship, says Maslow.

## Summary of the Chapter

In summary, the "Three Stools" approach involves three driving forces of our personality:

o   The Thinking part of who we are.
o   The Emotional part of who we are.
o   A third part that is an outgrowth of the first two: the Wants and Needs that arise in us.

The Three Stools, therefore, are Thinking, Emotions, and Wants/Needs. Each is described in the next chapter.

> Remember as you read the next chapter that you are being invited to connect with your inner Self, and by doing so, you will be better able to connect with your partner. By choosing which stool to "sit on" when interacting with your partner, you can greatly aid your relationship.

Discovery consists of looking at the same thing as everyone else and thinking something different.

Albert Szent-Gyorgyi
Nobel Prize for Medicine, 1937

54

# Chapter 6
# Sitting on Each Stool
-How to Be True to Yourself-

*"Trouble is part of your life, and if you don't share it, you don't give the person who loves you enough chance to love you enough."*

Dinah Shore
1916–1994, singer, television personality; immigrant parents; sociology degree from Vanderbilt; failed with major bands but became famous solo singer; married actor and artist George Montgomery, two children.

In *Hamlet* Shakespeare wrote:

*"This above all: To thine own self be true;
And it must follow, as the night the day,
Thou canst not then be false to any man."*

In these words, Shakespeare expressed amazing insight into human nature. To "be true" to oneself means being aware of one's thoughts, including one's opinions, judgments, and viewpoints; being aware of one's emotions; and being aware of one's wants and needs. If a person can be aware of these and express them to others, they will be expressing their own internal truth, and cannot "be false to any man."

"To thine own self be true" is easy to say, but often unbelievably difficult to perform, especially for those consciously trying for the first time. Yet it is the essence of emotional and relationship growth. Being true to oneself is essential.

## Sitting on the Thinking Stool

The Thinking Stool in this conversation model means analytical thinking. Here we find our opinions, viewpoints, judgments, perspectives, explanations, solutions, plans, logical deductions, problem solving, reporting, criticisms, and the like. The Thinking Stool is not about *all* mental or cognitive processes, which include formation of concepts, generation of speech, conversion of words and languages, visual construction, memory processes and levels, learning processes and mechanisms, and much more.

For example, all of the following are spoken from the Thinking Stool:

- o "This town has no interesting restaurants." (opinion)
- o "The table looks much better in that corner." (viewpoint)
- o "He can't be trusted, ever." (judgment)
- o "The reason he does that is it is all he knows." (explanation)
- o "Put the glasses on the top rack or they will break." (solution)
- o "We will leave in the early morning to be there by noon." (plan)
- o "When I said that, it caused him to change his mind, which led to ..." (logic)
- o "Bring six. That way we will have a spare in case ..." (problem solving)
- o "Let's build a new restaurant in town!" (plan)
- o "The kids did a great job!" (positive criticism)
- o "Six people were in that car, and none of them should have gone." (reporting, followed by viewpoint, opinion)

If these statements sound like those you encounter every day, you have a normal experience. We all say and hear these, or statements similar to them. We will see shortly, however, that relying on the Thinking Stool as the main speaking position in a relationship can easily create difficulties and become an underlying cause of hurtful, painful arguments.

Thinking—analytical thinking—is involved in building bridges, cars, phones, and planes; thinking writes scripts, songs, and plays; thinking has a part in painting, drawing, and sculpting. The Thinking Stool is certainly worth sitting on. It allows us to function every day in going to work, completing jobs, creating new things, and maintaining and organizing existing things. We cannot be without it.

But the Thinking Stool has one primary difficulty in relationships: it is the only one of the three from which a couple can argue. In other words, if you see a couple in a heated, circular, unending, perhaps yelling argument, you can be virtually certain that both are occupying the Thinking Stool. And, interestingly, they most likely do not understand that they are; nor do they understand how to move off of it or how to repair the relationship. Usually the couple will shut down or ignore the issue long enough for the subject to gradually fade into the past. They will not have learned how to prevent it from happening again. Further, the ghost or shadow of that argument and the hurt feelings around it will likely linger. Such grey shadows, when not recognized and addressed, make repairing and growing a relationship difficult.

If the Thinking Stool is the place of arguments, then we can expect that the Styles of Arguing discussed earlier in Chapter 1 have the Thinking Stool underlying them. For convenience, the Styles of

Arguing and examples of each are repeated here. Added to each example is a suggestion of a Thinking-based category that is likely in play.

### Types of Arguing Positions

*Intellectualize:*
"*That makes no sense at all. It is not logical.*" *(Or)* "*I can give you ten reasons why I'm right!*"
(judgment, logical deduction—as viewed by the speaker)

*Near Perfection:*
"*I am right, you are wrong, and everyone knows it but you.*"
(opinion, viewpoint)

*Denial:*
"*I did not do it.*" *(Or)* "*That did not happen, ever.*"
(explanation—as viewed by the speaker)

*Rejection:*
"*I don't care what you think. I'm leaving.*" *(Or)* "*I want you to go, now.*" (solution, plan—as viewed by the speaker)

*Exaggerate:*
"*You never get it right. You can't remember anything and you don't want to.*" *(Or)* "*You always, always, always say you will be on time and you never mean any of it.*" (opinion, judgment)

*Sarcasm:*
"*Sure, like everything else you do.*" *(Or)* "*Go ahead, interrupt me, I don't mind.*" (negative criticism, judgment)

*Blame:*
"*You started it. I did nothing.*" (judgment, opinion)

For each argumentative statement, there is a category of thinking or thought that applies, as shown in parentheses. Further, the statement can often be recognized as the judgment or opinion of the speaker. It is their truth, as they perceive it. Note, however,

58

that in each statement above there is no sign of ownership by the speaker. Instead, each statement is presented as if everyone knows it is true, as if it is a universal truth that only the listener is unaware of. To make this point even stronger, note that after each statement above, you could write "Dummy!" and that is what the listener likely perceives. For example:

*Blame:*
*"You started it. I did nothing. Dummy!"*

So, please look at each statement above, add the word "Dummy" at the end, and imagine the sound of the sentence.

Well, here we have it. Thinking Stool statements can, in some tense situations, be taken as telling the other person that they are a "dummy." The message to the listener can be that everyone else knows the truth, the speaker is the only correct person between the two of them, and the listener is simply wrong.

Remember the previous section on invalidation? How the arguing styles have in common an invalidation of our partner in an attempt to defend our inner Self? That these arguments are often the result of someone first feeling "set-aside," rejected," "put down," or "dismissed"? We can link all of this together. We can now delineate that opinions, judgments, viewpoints, and the like made from the Thinking Stool can lead to our partner feeling invalidated, which leads to defenses and even aggression, which leads to the arguments and verbal attacks.

As mentioned earlier, arguments only occur on the Thinking Stool, and now we can understand how this occurs. No doubt you have experienced this linear progression yourself:

o   First …   Someone makes a statement that upsets you.

o   Second …Your reaction happens quickly and without warning.

o   Third … The argument takes off like an exploding rocket.

Importantly, if you look back at your experience with this progression, the upsetting statement was very likely one from the analytical thinking category, such as an opinion, a judgment, or a plan of action. Further, that statement was likely said in such a way that you felt dismissed, with the result that you quickly, perhaps instantly, became angry. If you acted on that anger in an aggressive way, either verbally or physically, in order to defend yourself, you probably acted dismissively to the other person, which angered them, and the argument rocket exploded off the launch pad. The beginning of this explosion was the Thinking Stool—the very same stool that is so important for daily talking, creativity, progress, and change.

At this point you may be experiencing some confusion, which might go something like this:

> OK, analytical thinking statements occur all the time; we all say them. They comprise most of our speech. They are critical to what we do, what we create, and what we plan to do. Yet I see that analytical statements can be at the root of an argument. They can imply invalidation of my partner, and that leads to hurt feelings and arguments. So, what am I to do?

Should I:

- Not give my opinions to my partner? Just keep quiet?
  - *Answer: No, this is not a viable solution. We want relationship, not isolation.*

- Give my viewpoints and plans and thoughts, but be sure they line up with my partner's viewpoints, in order to avoid an argument?
  - *Answer: No, this is not a viable approach either.*

- Give my opinions the way I always have and if my partner feels invalidated, then that's too bad? We can fight about it and maybe they will see my point?
  - *Answer: This is likely where you are now, and not where you want to be.*

- Give my opinion, being careful that I recognize and validate my partner during the conversation. Recognize their opinions, plans, and thoughts while explaining my own, so we can somehow find a way to share and both feel included?
  - *Answer: This is the path that works. We will be discussing more on ways to achieve this in a later section.*

The Thinking Stool is essential in our lives, but we need to be careful that we do not diminish those close to us as we express our opinions, plans, and directives. Statements that essentially pronounce that no further discussion is expected may be perfectly in order and effective at work ... but not at home. Not in committed relationships. To invite and to grow relationships, we can have our opinions, but we must leave room for the thoughts and opinions of the other person. Validation matters greatly in relationships. We must be careful not to imply "dummy" at the

61

end of our statements. *We must own our opinions as ours*, pointing out, "I may be mistaken, but this is my viewpoint, my opinion, my judgment." This would be an example of "To thine own self be true." A judgment owned by the speaker can never be called wrong and does not imply "dummy," while a judgment stated as if it is fact may indeed be wrong and has the potential to greatly offend.

## Sitting on the Emotions Stool

Emotions—your feelings—can be expressed as *single words*, such as "happy," "sad," and "angry." Before we begin a description of this facet of effective conversation, here is an experiment:

> *Make a list of all the emotions you know. Before reading further, simply take a piece of paper and write all that come to mind. Or, use the lines below.*

*(Please do not read beyond this line until you have made a list, at least a mental list, of emotions you know and have counted them. Thank you.)*

_____

_____

_____

_____

_____

How many emotions did you list? _____

The Emotions Stool is covered with small pieces of paper, each containing a single word; each an emotion, a feeling. Here is a short list of such single words. Note that the hyphenated words are considered single:

Joyful, happy, ecstatic, glad, serene, curious, inquisitive, moody, out-of-sorts, unhappy, depressed, heartbroken, put-aside, sad, worried, anxious, doubtful, timid, upset, fearful, chicken, alarmed, skeptical, confused, uncertain, excited, bold, secure, daring, youthful, and zany.

*More emotion words are listed in alphabetical order in Appendix 2, "Feeling Words."*

Over two thousand feeling words have been listed on various websites and in various books. Typically, however, people only able to list a few emotions. How many did you list? My experience is that six or seven is average for a first list; twenty is exceptional. We have the situation, therefore, that people *undergo* many emotions, their limbic systems (Chapter 4) generate many, yet they are often *readily aware* of only a few. In other words, they are not in touch with how they are feeling and what is going on inside them. Are you one such person? If so, welcome to a very large population of people who, likewise, are not fully in touch with their inner selves and with their emotions.

We can be out of touch with our feelings for a variety of reasons, such as learning in childhood to automatically bury feelings, or simply never trying or learning to recognize and honor feelings. Certainly a child who is told "Don't cry," may become an adult who views crying as a weakness and who buries their emotions, even, for example, at the funeral of a friend. In fact, the "Don't cry" instruction they received as a child may have been made at a funeral.

Further, we all are adept at finding ways to avoid feeling our emotions, especially if feeling them creates discomfort in us.

These various methods of avoidance are referred to as "defense mechanisms" or simply "defenses." These defenses keep our feelings at a distance. People overindulge in alcohol, work overtime, shut down, or begin to act-out with anger, to name a few defenses. Freud identified many defenses, including denial, distortion of reality, aggression, displacement of anger to something else, suppression of feelings, and more.

Having emotions and being aware of them are separate events. Yet, for relationships to grow, awareness is crucial. The Emotions Stool must be used. And it certainly cannot be worn out; it offers an endless supply of feelings, often the same feelings repeating over time. But as the relationship grows, the feelings will change; that change is one sign of growth. Frustration, for example, can be replaced more often with feelings of peace, connection, and support. Loneliness, hurt, and anger can be reversed.

Now that we can recognize feelings as describable with single words, we can be careful with our expression of feelings. In particular, people will "sit on" the Thinking Stool to make comments which they claim are their feelings. Further, by claiming that they are expressing their feelings, they will also claim a right to express themselves, even if they are being attacking and invalidating to the other person. As you can imagine, none of this is helpful for a relationship, but it is not intended—not usually. Instead, the person claiming that they are simply expressing their emotions truly does not know that they are actually being judgmental, opinionated, or invalidating of the other person. They are unaware.

In the example that follows, the speaker might well say "I am just expressing my feelings," when in fact what follows is a sentence, not a single word that describes a feeling. The result is analytical thought poorly masquerading as feelings. Further, we will witness in this example the kind of analytical thought described earlier as causing trouble and leading to arguments. Here is the example:

> "I *feel* that Josh and Sam must come with us, otherwise they will certainly get lost out there."

This statement can easily come across to the listener, the speaker's partner, as a judgment. It is certainly not a feeling; it is a long sentence, not a single word. Further, if the *listener* had a different plan, the possibility of being disregarded might loom, and an argument might ensue. In particular, the listener's reply might be:

> "They won't get lost! Don't be silly. They can go on their own."

This conversation may be off to a very bad beginning.

If, however, the first person had said what they were *actually feeling*, the conversation could take a productive path. The true feeling statement might have been:

> "I am *concerned*. I *worry* that if Josh and Sam don't come with us, they might get lost out there."

Be careful when talking with your partner that you call feelings "feelings," and thoughts (opinions, judgments, viewpoints, plans, et cetera) what they actually are, that is, "thoughts." Doing so is the first step to productive conversations with your partner, and to improved connection and intimacy.

Finally, let's recall the main point of this section: that being aware of one's feelings is often difficult but is also vital for relationships to flourish. Be on—and talk from—the Emotions Stool as often as possible as a gift to yourself and to others. Your connection, clarity, and understanding with your partner, family member, child, or friend can only improve. Further, if the other person works on hearing you and on expressing their emotions, your relationship will take on new dimensions. More will be discussed later on how to carry on such a dialogue.

## Sitting on the Wants and Needs Stool

Virtually all of us have wants, needs, goals, likes and dislikes, wishes, and dreams. The purpose of this third stool is to further assist in having productive and truly connecting conversations with your partner (or a family member, or a friend, or ...). We have discussed that the Thinking Stool can create difficulties when comments are made in such a way as to create an attacking atmosphere, or when a sense of invalidation is felt by either person. We must take care to own our thoughts, opinions, and judgments. We have discussed the value of the Emotions Stool in allowing us and our partners to better understand what is occurring inside of us: what we are feeling. The third stool of Wants and Needs is likewise important and offers its own gift for a relationship.

Knowing what we want "should" be easy. But it is not. It is hard enough to know, sometimes, what we want for dinner, or what movie we want to see, or what shoes we want to wear. Knowing what we want or need for our internal, emotional well-being is often even more difficult, probably because we are not practiced at thinking about it or asking for it. When we were children, our parents may not have listened well to our requests. "Mom, I need Johnny to stop poking me" may have fallen on tired ears, or, "Dad,

I want to go to the game with you" may not have been understood with the same craving with which it was said. Now, in committed relationships, we have the opportunity to express our wants, needs, wishes, and dreams, but the opportunity easily eludes us; we are not accustomed to knowing, let alone asking. To be able to speak from the Wants and Needs Stool, we have to practice being in touch with our own internal wants and needs. Further, we have to begin changing our conversation from directing, or expecting, or complaining, to more frequently expressing what we would like.

The table on the next page compares speaking from the Wants and Needs Stool to speaking in an ineffective way. The table labels these two ways as "Old Way" and "New Way." The advantages of expressing one's own wishes ... the "New Way" ... are that:

- You express your own internal world of what is important to you.

- You do not attack or diminish the other person.

- Your partner learns more about you.

- You learn more about yourself.

- Each statement is true and honest.

- Each statement is not a judgment or a command.

| Old Way | New Way |
| --- | --- |
| "I expect you to be on time; you are not reliable!" | "I need you to be on time. This is important to me. I need you to be reliable." |
| "Just keep quiet. Get out of the room." | "I need some space and quiet right now. I am saturated. I <u>do</u> want to talk, but later." |
| "You started this. I didn't say a word!" | "I want us to be closer. This argument is not what I want. I would like to start this conversation again." |
| "Fifty-six dollars! You think money grows on trees!" | "I would like to get that for you, but I cannot right now. I need your help to find something a little less costly." |
| "I've told you one hundred times, put the knives in the drawer with the sharp edge down!" | "It is important to me to have the sharp edge of the knives down; that's just how I am." |
| "When we go to parties you leave me with strangers. Stop it! You can't just walk away!" | "I do not like being with people I don't know at these parties. I need you to introduce me to them, and sometimes to stay with me rather than walking off. It is important to me." |

After reading the above examples, many people say, "I can do that, it will be easy." But my experience in working with people over the years shows that it is not so easy.

For example, in attempting to contact their own inner Self, and to express needs, dreams, wishes, et cetera, people will simply soften how they express the "Old Way," the left column on the previous page. Instead of making an argumentative statement such as the first one on the previous page,

> "I expect you to be on time. You are not reliable."

they believe an improvement in their approach is,

> "I do not get it. You are late again. We agreed on six o'clock!"

They are not being clear about *their own needs*, but they often think they are being clear. Notice from the table that a clear statement, one that may challenge their partner and is straightforward and honest, is,

> "I need you to be on time. This is important to me. I need you to be reliable."

Or, as another example of how it is difficult to automatically express needs appropriately, a person might be saying what the other person "should do" or "should understand," but misrepresent their viewpoint as a "need" or "want":

> "I want you to see that this is your fault!"
> "I need you to see that you don't get it!"

These statements are inappropriate and not helpful. Remember that your goal is to be all the way into the right-hand column above. Also remember that to do so is not automatic and not as easy as it may seem. Practice. Keep trying.

This time, like all times, is a very good one, if we but know what to do with it.

Ralph Waldo Emerson

# Chapter 7
# Barriers

*"We must become the change we want to see."*

Mahatma Gandhi
1869–1948, Indian philosopher, internationally esteemed for his doctrine of nonviolent protest, was a major political and spiritual leader of India and leader of the Indian independence movement.

By changing in order to better connect with ourselves—yes, with ourselves—and then taking that better understanding of how we feel and what we need or want in the moment and expressing those internal connections to our partner (or family member, or close friend), we can grow. The growth can be not only in better understanding who we are and in our capabilities, but in the relationship as well. Couples and families can find amazing, heartfelt, deep, and loving growth. But change and growth are often a bit scary … uncomfortable … unfamiliar. There are barriers to our willingness to change and to grow.

Two conditions need to occur within each of us for our connection with others to be strong. First, we must be aware of what is going on within ourselves, which is the meaning of that Shakespeare line, "To thine own self be true." Second, we must be willing to express ourselves: to talk. People struggle with both of these. We have barriers, probably mostly subconscious, that interfere with

71

our own awareness and our willingness to talk. To be more effective with our partners, and to grow to our fullest potential, therefore, we can benefit from understanding something about our own barriers and from learning to walk around or climb over them. Here are some examples of barriers ...

## Myth: Weaklings Cry

If we have been told, or if we perceive that we were told, that crying is unacceptable and that "babies cry," we may view contact with our emotions as a sign of weakness or believe that it is unacceptable within the family. The barrier is our own misjudgment that "stopping to feel emotions is weakness." Another misjudgment and barrier is saying to ourselves, "Crying, even crying inside myself, is weakness and it only creates more of a problem." The real truth is that courage and strength are required to make contact with our emotions, whether we are male or female.

## Myth: Acting-Out with Anger Helps

If we learn at a young age that yelling, screaming, waving our arms, stomping, slamming doors, et cetera, create a defense that protects us from losing during an argument, we may come to rely on that behavior as the only tool we know. This behavior is usually first learned at two to four years old when another child takes a toy or pushes into the line waiting for the sliding board. By the time we are 20 or 30 or 40, we may not have learned another approach, in which case we only know the one way we learned that worked for us on the playground. The barrier to using the "Three Stools" approach is our misjudgment that "fighting back is the best and fastest way to stop the other person from invalidating me." The difficulty, of course, is that as adults, mean and hurtful fighting prevents us from having the very relationship we crave. In addition, our partner never comes to truly understand us.

# Myth: Rage Rocks

If we learn at a young age that throwing objects, punching walls, and generally scaring or threatening the other person with verbal and physical abuse is the effective way to "win," then that behavior can become a habit. The raging adult gains the center of attention and takes control. Too many people have this explosive, uncontrolled behavior, and many dislike themselves for doing it. Conversely, some teenagers, unfortunately, are finding satisfaction by posting videos of their own raging behavior on the Internet; they view themselves as instant movie stars. Raging is a behavior that can lead to legal issues and separation rather than a closer relationship. The barrier, if we practice raging as a tool to win, is our misjudgment that "raging will instantly give me control and make this right." The great difficulty is that a raging person can cause physical and emotional harm. Healthy relationships cannot exist in such an environment.

# Myth: Pushing-Away is Best

Pushing-away means to avoid contacting our own thoughts, emotions, wants, and needs out of a belief, perhaps subconscious, that to do so will be unproductive and perhaps even harmful to the relationship. This belief is basically one that convinces us, when we are upset in any way, that avoiding any contact with our true feelings and thoughts is the safest and surest approach to healing the relationship. Pushing-back takes the form of ...

- o Watching excessive television with the purpose of avoiding the issues.

- o Shutting down on your partner or family member.

- o Telling jokes to divert hurtful issues.

o Taking on many tasks or many activities again, as a diversion.

o Directing loving attention to someone else in the family, even the pet dog, to form a closer bond with them rather than connecting with one's partner through discussion of the emotions and needs each has.

The barrier is the misjudgment that "avoiding this situation is best and this will … like a kidney stone … pass. Just give it a little time." Pushing-away and avoiding creates a missed opportunity.

## Not a Myth: Depression

The subject of depression is complex, wide, deep, and beyond the scope of this book, but a brief discussion has a place here for two reasons. First, depression is a barrier to emotions, and second, using the "Three Stools" approach can be useful as a first step to helping someone find help for depression: not the only first step possible, but a useful one.

Depression has many levels of severity and takes on many forms, from feeling "blue" or somewhat down, to having no interest in normally pleasant activities, and to the extreme of feeling nearly hopeless about the future. Further, depression can sometimes be discerned by observing a person's behavior, such as major changes in eating and sleeping patterns, fatigue, confusion, disinterest in activities, and perhaps self-medicating with alcohol. On the other hand, depression can be covert, or hidden, which is believed to be more prominent in men than women. With covert depression the person may continue to be functional; executives, for example, continue to run companies well, but they feel empty and often hide their symptoms. Work, in fact, may be the one place they feel the most appreciated and the least empty.

Depression can be present for short periods of time, or can last for years. It can be prompted by family genetics, or it can be solely situational to events and stressful issues. Clearly, if you or someone you know has signs of depression, help from a therapist or psychiatrist is vital. Depression affects relationships greatly, and it can lead to harmful actions. But depression can be treated; so please be certain to seek help.

Depression creates a barrier to dialogue and connection with a partner. Depression interferes with a person's ability to both experience joy and access emotions. Depression coats a person's normal process of generating a variety of emotions—frustration, exuberance, fear, acceptance, and even love—with a gray paint of disinterest. If a couple wants to work on their relationship with the "Three Stools" approach, connection with their emotions, needs, wants, and thoughts is necessary. Depression renders that connection difficult.

Not all is lost, however. Depression can be addressed within the relationship. As a caring couple, or as a caring family member or friend, whatever your meaningful relationship is, talking about the depression with your partner is important. Whether you suspect that *they* are depressed or that *you* are depressed, talk about it. Further, use the tools of the "Three Stools" approach to talk about it. While depression interferes with accessing emotions and thoughts, a slow, caring dialogue can be a life-changing experience. The goal of such a dialogue, if someone indeed is depressed, is to agree on a plan for talking with a professional.

Here are a few summary points concerning depression:

- Can be mild or severe, or any level in between.
- Can be difficult to detect; people pretend they are fine.
- Can be related to family genetics.
- Can be triggered by some traumatic situation.
- Can interfere with one's ability to think clearly.
- Can interfere with accessing one's full range of emotions.
- Is often ignored by people as if it is a normal state of living and one they think they need to accept.
- Is often an embarrassment to people, so they choose not to discuss it and they do not understand why it is happening to them.
- Carries with it feelings of hopelessness, confusion, helplessness, and even anxiety.
- Occurs in one out of five people at some point in their life.
- Is treatable.

## Not a Myth: Anxiety

A discussion of barriers would not be complete without mentioning the effects of anxiety. While anxiety and depression present very differently in people—the first being more like nervousness, and the second generally, not always, displaying as sluggishness and lack of interest—the two are like close cousins; they often travel together. Whether anxiety or depression occurs first depends on the person, and sometimes they do not occur together; a person may be only depressed or only anxious. One person will say, "Ignoring my anxiety for years caused me social problems and that led to depression." Yet another will say, "I was so depressed that I did nothing and I began to be confused and anxious about what would happen to me and my kids." Others may show only signs of depression or only signs of anxiety.

Anxiety has many levels. It can be mild, or nearly debilitating, or any level in between. One common effect is that it can cause confusion and interfere with clear thinking and clear understanding. Since it can be a barrier to connecting with your emotions, wants, needs, and thoughts, anxiety can prevent you from having a close and meaningful dialogue with another person. Therefore, being aware of your own or someone else's level of anxiety is important if you are attempting to make a connection. Teenagers, for example, may have difficulty hearing a parent's repeated and frustrated requests to "be on time," or "get ready for dinner, please," if they are feeling high anxiety over an ensuing test, a cheerleading tryout, a first date, or a dress or shirt they can't find. Anxiety, like depression, can fog the mind and prevent clear focus.

Here are a few summary points concerning anxiety:
o   Can be mild or severe, or any level in between.
o   Can be always present.
o   Can be present only during certain situations.
o   Can be related to family genetics.
o   Can be triggered by some traumatic situation.
o   Can interfere with one's ability to think clearly and to mentally focus.
o   Can interfere with accessing one's true thoughts and emotions.
o   Is often ignored by people as if it is a normal state of being and one they think they need to accept.
o   Is often an embarrassment to people, so they choose not to discuss it and they do not understand why it is happening to them.
o   Creates an inability to think straight, remain focused, and cope with various situations.
o   Is believed to be the most common mental health issue, counting all forms of anxiety from social anxiety to panic.
o   Is treatable.

If you or someone you know may have anxiety, seek professional help. Also, talk about it with your partner. Speak from the heart.

## Chapter Summary

In summary, the effort needed to climb over our own barriers to achieving improved communications and improved relationships with those we want close in our lives involves an effort of awareness, expression, and listening. How to do these better is expanded in chapters that follow.

Extra effort is needed to be conscious of our barriers, and extra effort is required to be aware of our internal emotions, needs, and thoughts. We must encourage ourselves in a highly conscious way to sit on each of the three stools, and to speak and to listen from each stool, until the process becomes more automatic, more unconscious.

The effort lies in purposely working in a conscious way to be aware of one's inner Self, even if the experience is at first uncomfortable. If the process feels stressful or highly unfamiliar, then seeking professional help, at least for a short time, is highly advisable. The closeness you achieve with your partner and others can be an amazing and fulfilling experience.

# Chapter 8
# "Listen More Slowly"

*"People ought to listen more slowly!"*

Jean Sparks Ducey
Librarian and author of
children's books.

Listening is a gift to the person speaking. The speaker recognizes that the listener is setting their own emotions, wants, and needs aside in order to understand. Listening sends a message, a loud and clear message, as if the words were shouted. The loud and clear message is "I am listening because I care about you, and because I care about our relationship."

Learning to *speak* one's own inner truth of thoughts, feelings, wants, and needs requires great effort, practice, and an awareness of barriers, as discussed in previous chapters. But speaking is only half the effort. The other half, equally as difficult, is *listening*. Not just listening to hear the words, but listening to understand, to feel, and to internalize the emotions behind the words you hear.

*"One friend, one person who is truly understanding, who takes the trouble to listen to us as we consider our problems, can change our whole outlook."*

Elton Mayo
1880–1949, Australian psychologist, professor at University of Queensland, University of Pennsylvania, and Harvard Business School. Landmark study of worker relationships at Western Electric in the 1920s.

Listening, true listening, requires energy; it is not a passive job. A listener who hears and seeks to understand exerts energy. True listening requires a curious and caring person, one who will use every quiet effort they can find to enter the inner world of the person speaking. The efforts and energies for true listening occur in two basic ways:

- Focusing
- Paraphrasing

## Focusing

Focusing involves using one's energies to avoid distractions, to concentrate, and to internalize the words, thoughts, emotions, and expressed needs of the person talking. Focusing is perhaps the most important effort, since the next steps of paraphrasing, connecting, and clarifying depend entirely on how well one has heard, understood, and attempted to assimilate the message of the person talking. Focusing involves looking at the person talking, noticing their expressions, and mentally recording the messages in their words and in their expressions. Focusing also involves turning off the television, asking the kids to go outside, moving to within a few feet of the person speaking, and setting aside all chatter in one's mind about what happened at work or about how to defend one's self against the *perceived* blame that might be coming.

In summary, when your partner (friend, family member, et cetera) is attempting to express to you their inner world of *their* Three Stools, your first effort as a true listener is to focus. Focusing simply requires that you exert effort in these ways:

o Look at the person talking.
o Be fairly close to them.
o Turn of the television; turn off your cell phone; say in advance that you will not answer the home phone; close the door.
o Ask the person talking to help you focus by allowing you to interrupt their story after they have given you one or two "chunks" of information. The interruption will be for you to paraphrase back, which is discussed below. If too much is said before you paraphrase back, the line of thought can become confusing.
o Mentally record the messages you are hearing. Prepare for paraphrasing, which comes next. Mentally make note of what is not clear so you can ask later. Ask now if you must know in order to understand the situation. In order to avoid interrupting, ask later if you can wait.
o Turn off any chatter in your mind. This includes chatter that may arise about how to argue back to point out how the person speaking is somehow wrong. Remember, they are, in this situation, expressing what is true for them: Three Stools. This is not an argument.
o Hear their words and how they say them. Listen with your ears *and* your eyes. Look at their face, their body, and their hands. Try to understand the emotions and the messages they are feeling and

sending physically. (Perhaps review Chapter 4 and the section on emotions affecting physical behavior.)

o   Let them know you are with them in their story. Give indications that you understand as they are talking. If you do not, either ask for clarification at the moment, or wait for an appropriate break.

## Paraphrasing

The value of saying back, or paraphrasing, to the other person your summary of what you heard is that it confirms for them that you received the message as they meant it. If you did not understand it as they meant it, then clarification can be made. Further, as they hear you repeat the message, it reinforces and clarifies it for them. Their own message takes on more life because they hear you say it. You do not have to agree with their viewpoint, but in sharing it with you they will very likely feel more accepted. This separation of the content of a discussion from the validation of the person is the point made in Chapter 3 when describing the "two-rung ladder" model of arguments.

Paraphrasing has two components. One is repeating back the content, the actual story and information, which your partner is attempting to make clear to you. Your job in paraphrasing is to repeat that story and information back to them to show that you heard it and you understand it.

The second component of paraphrasing is conveying and honoring the underlying emotions of the person speaking. This is not about the content, but it may be the stronger message that your partner wants you to understand. Your job is to show your partner that you have a sense of the emotions they are experiencing or that they had experienced in the situation they are discussing. Your partner may not say they are frustrated, or sad, or confused, or lonely, but your job as a true listener is to be a detective. Your job is to attempt to discern their underlying feelings. Emotional closeness and intimacy depend upon a capacity for empathy. During the paraphrasing, you can suggest that you sense a frustration, or some other emotion, and ask if that is correct. Explore what your partner is feeling and help them understand themselves. Remember, showing your partner that you are aware of their emotions and underlying messages, and that you understand or at least are trying to understand, is the primary value of paraphrasing.

In summary, here are a few tips for paraphrasing what you hear from your partner:

o Point out in advance to your partner that you will be repeating back, in your own words, what you hear, and that you would like to repeat back after they have given you one or two "chunks" of information. Point out that this will probably mean you have to interrupt them so you can give feedback.

o When paraphrasing, keep it short. This will require that you listen closely and process the information as you listen, as discussed in the Focusing section above.

o Repeat back, in your own words, the story and information you heard.

o Describe the emotions that you sensed or heard during your listening. Empathize with your partner, but not in a mechanical way. Dig deep into your own emotions. Imagine how they are feeling, or had been feeling during the situation they are describing. Let them know how much of that you understand. Again, empathize.

o After paraphrasing, ask if what you said was correct and if it was complete for those one or two "chunks." Be curious. If your partner says, "Not quite correct," be open to correction and paraphrase back the correct message once you understand it.

o   After paraphrasing, ask "What else?" In other words, "What is the next 'chunk' of information?" Again, be curious.

## Example of "Listening More Slowly"

The following example demonstrates the key points of an effective dialogue in a relationship. A more involved example can be found in Chapter 10.

In this fictional example, Megan and Matthew have two children, Will, age six, and Lorie, age four. Megan has chosen not to work in order to be with the children in all of their various activities. She does, however, spend many hours volunteering at the school library. In striving to be a "good" mom and a supportive partner for Matthew, she sometimes feels overwhelmed. Matthew works in the city, which is an hour's drive away, in a job that can be highly demanding.

The following effective and constructive dialogue between Megan and Matthew will show how they express themselves and how they listen ... really listen. *Two basic skill sets* are being used by the couple in this example:

1.   The couple is using the "Three Stools." They are "owning," that is, being aware of and taking responsibility for, (a) their opinions and thoughts; (b) their emotions; and (c) their wants and needs.

In the following dialogue, the words reflecting a, b, and c are italicized.

84

2. They practice focusing and paraphrasing.

As the scene opens on this couple, the day is Saturday and the time is around noon. Will is reading his favorite book on birds, while younger Lorie has fallen asleep after hours of spinning in her dance dress and her magic shoes. Matthew looks for Megan and finds her in the kitchen reading a recipe ...

> Matthew enters the kitchen, pulling up a chair near Megan. He *does not want* to interrupt her train of thought about the recipe, so he waits. When she looks up at him he says, "I *need* to talk about something that has been *bothering* me for a week."
>
> Megan puts down the cookbook, replying, "OK. I can sit with you now. Or later if that is better for you."
>
> Matthew *appreciates* her willingness and responds, "Good. Thanks. Now is good. *I don't think* this will take too long." He is a little *nervous* but tries not to show it. He is *hoping* this will not turn into hurt feelings or an argument.
>
> Megan says, "I can ask Will to watch a video for a while. Lorie will be sleeping. So, we should be fine."
>
> Megan goes to the other room, where she sets up a video for Will, who is thrilled.
>
> Megan and Matthew go to the nearby spare bedroom to talk, a place they have decided is neutral and will not remind them of any fights they have had. Nor is it their own bedroom, which they have decided is off-limits for tense discussions or discussions about work.
>
> Matthew sits next to Megan on the bed and begins by saying, "OK. First, I *want* to say that this is not something

really serious. I did not lose my job or anything. It has to do with you and me."

Megan looks a little relieved as she replies, "OK."

Matthew continues by saying, "And I *want* you to know that I *love* you and our family, but I just *need* to tell you something."

Megan replies, "OK. I'm ready to listen. And I *want* to repeat back what I have heard you say, so I might have to slow you down a bit."

Matthew says, "Fine. I *appreciate* that. It's a good idea."

Matthew begins by saying, "First, *thanks* for taking the time. This is what *I need* to talk about: I am *upset* about *my view*—I own it—of how you have been acting when I come home after work. I work my tail off and when I get home its like the lid is blown off the place. I *feel* like I'm *going nuts*, plus I can't talk to you when I get home."

Megan has been watching Matthew as he talks. She sees the pained look on his face, and the nervous way he moves around on the bed. She also notices her own defensive reaction to Matthew's words, "I am upset with how you have been acting." The word "you" jumps out at her. She *feels defensive* but quickly puts it aside. She *wants* to be in Matthew's inner world and involved in his concerns, not defend herself.

Megan *decides* to paraphrase now before she loses the message with more messages. She says, "OK, let me get this part. You are *upset* with me ... I mean, you are upset with how you view my actions when you get home and with the whole environment when you get home. It feels like the lid is blown off the place. Right?" Matthew nods "yes," so Megan continues. "And all of this make you feel like you are going nuts. What else?"

86

Matthew can feel his temperature lowering. He is more *relaxed*. His breathing is slowing down, and his words begin to slow as well. He takes a deep breath before continuing.

Megan notices that her husband is *calmer*, and notices that she is also calmer. She then focuses all of her attention back on Matthew.

Matthew continues, "I am *exhausted* when I get home. I *look forward* to getting here, but when I come in the door, I want to run. But I don't want to run. *I don't know*. It's *confusing*. All I know for sure is that something has to change. I try to say hello to you, to hold you a moment, but you avoid me. At least, that is how it seems to me. We both end up chasing the kids, and arguing about who did what, and trying to get the kids to sit at the dinner table. It's a mess." At this point Matthew realizes that Megan deals with this, too. He says, "I don't know how you do it ... all day."

Megan wants to respond to Matthew's observation that the household can be difficult for her, but she realizes the importance of staying with Matthew's concerns and his feelings, rather than suddenly switching to her issues.

Megan chooses to say, "I *think I hear* what you are saying. You are *exhausted* when you get home. You *want* to say hello to me, to be with me even if for a short time. You *want* some quiet, some peace, some rest. Right?" Matthew nods in agreement. "But instead you find chaos. You want to run and you don't want to run. It is confusing for you. You find yourself chasing after the kids, getting into arguments with them and maybe me, and you don't like it. Right?" Again, Matthew agrees. "And my guess is that when this happens you are angry. So, you come home and end up *tired, exhausted, and angry*. Is this right?"

87

Matthew says, "That's exactly right."

Megan asks, "What else?"

Matthew has a puzzled look as he says, "I don't know 'what else.' I just *wish* we could find another way. Have it be different."

Notice that through this conversation, Matthew is probably feeling close and connected to Megan. So, he is gaining the feeling of connection and of being cared about, the very emotion that he lacks when he comes home to chaos. Discussion of his feeling separate from Megan is pulling them together.

Megan senses that Matthew is complete for now, so she asks, "Can I express myself now? Are you done enough for now?"

Matthew says, "Sure. Absolutely." He is eager to hear how she feels and what she is dealing with in this chaotic household.

Megan says, "First, I feel really good hearing you talk about what is bothering you. It is *important to me* to know that you will tell me what is going on with you. Second, I am *exhausted*, too. Let's start with that. I am trying to keep this house fairly picked up and clean, I am chauffeuring the kids around to dance and piano and school and their friends' houses ... and I *feel like little pieces* are being torn out of me. I take care of you and them, and in the process, I feel as if I *disappear*. Like there is no 'me.' I hate that. I never—well, almost never—have time for myself. So when you get home, I..."

Matthew interrupts her, "Wait. Please hold that thought. You started to say, 'When you get home, I ...' Before you go on to that thought, I need to capture what you just said.

88

OK?" Megan agrees. "You are exhausted, you feel picked apart, you do for everyone else and have no time left for yourself. Right?" Megan agrees. "So, I am guessing ... and hearing ... that you are angry. You feel picked apart. Right?" Megan, again, agrees. "OK. I understand that. What else?"

Megan says, "When you get home, a hug would be nice. I *want* that, too. But I *guess my anger* gets in the way...and I am *stressed* out. I feel so *responsible* for everything." She falls back onto the bed, nearly crying under the weight of feeling so responsible and feeling no support during the day. Matthew notices her near tears.

Mathew notices her near tears. He reaches out to hold her hand, saying, "You want to be with me, too, when I get home, but the stress and anger get in the way. And you feel really responsible for holding everything together." Megan gets teary again just hearing him say the words. "I am sorry. I don't want you to feel this way."

Megan sits up and responds by looking at Matthew and saying quietly, "Thank you."

Matthew waits for a minute before asking, "Anything else?"

Megan says, "No. I just want this to be different, too. This is not working the way either of us would like."

Matthew nods and says, "I agree."

Neither of them talks for a while. Each waits to see if the other person has more to say about what is bothering them.

After a few minutes of silence, Matthew says, "Can we start to address some changes we can make for ourselves?"

Megan smiles slightly for the first time, responding, "Sure!" She is feeling a little hopeful and continues to show it in her face.

At this point the dialogue changes from one of describing, sharing, hearing, and understanding the problem to one of finding a solution.

In this solution mode, the couple discusses small but significant changes that will work for them. Matthew agrees that he will call every day on his way home to talk with Megan about what is happening and what she may need when he gets home. If necessary, he will pick up something from the store on the way home as a way of supporting her, so she feels a little less responsible for having all the shopping done. Also, Matthew tells Megan that when he gets home each evening he will pick up toys from all over the house and he will make a game out of it with Will and Lorie. They agree that Megan does not have to feel responsible for having the place looking perfect when Matthew gets home. They agree that the first thing they will do is take five minutes for themselves when Matthew walks in the door. Matthew agrees with Megan when she says, "The kids can do something on their own for five or ten minutes while we have our time."

They continue the discussion, coming up with small but creative ways to support each other and to feel connected. The couple discusses how to arrange a family dinner each night, handle bathtime for the kids, read bedtime stories, and more. They plan to work together as a team. In the end, the children end up being included in the connection: Matthew and Megan play more with the kids, and Matthew makes a game out of cleaning up the toys.

All of this extended sense of teamwork, mutual caring, mutual support, shared understanding, connection, and time with each other and with the children came from one well executed concept: Matthew and Megan decided to TALK with each other.

While it is simple to say, "We will talk with each other," actually talking and being effective is difficult for the reasons discussed in the earlier chapters of this book. Yet a step-by-step commitment to progress in the "Three Stools" approach can lead to the type of discussion Matthew and Megan experienced.

The next chapter provides an overall summary of all the skills involved in this communications journey.

You may see things and say "Why?"
But I dream things that never were
and say "Why not?"

George Bernard Shaw

# Chapter 9
## "Three Stools" Summary
### with
## Integration of the Tools

*"We must be our own before we can be another's."*

*Ralph Waldo Emerson*
1803–1882, New England essayist, philosopher, poet, captivating orator whose father called him "dull" at age eight; graduated Harvard at age twenty-two.

Here is a summary in outline form. This summary begins by reaching back into the Introduction and the points discussed there, then travels through the concepts and ideas of each of the "Three Stools" and of "Listening More Slowly."

## What Are the "Three Stools"?

- The "Three Stools" are Thinking, Emotions, and Wants/Needs. Each will be described in more detail below. Remember as you read that you are being invited to connect with your inner-self, and that by doing so, you will be better able to connect with your partner. By choosing which stool to "sit on" when interacting with your partner, you can greatly aid your relationship.

# Who Can Be Helped by the "Three Stools" Approach

- The overall objective of this communication approach is to allow and facilitate connection and closeness between two people in a caring relationship.
  - o The primary relationship addressed here is a couple in a committed relationship, but it may also be two family members, such as a parent and a teenage child, or an adult and one of their parents. This book often uses the word "partner" for the other person in your relationship; it is simply a shorthand that can be replaced with "significant other," "teenager," "parent," "brother or sister," or "close and caring friend."
  - o For full effectiveness, both people must be willing to explore their own inner-selves. This may be difficult for some adults, and certainly can be difficult for teenagers, since they are still maturing. Commitment to beginning is the key. With some positive results, people are more willing to continue.
  - o Even if a partner is unwilling or less able to engage in this dialogue of expressing themselves clearly, definite improvement can be noticed in a relationship if one person learns and practices the approach. Plus, this way of addressing issues often feels more honest to the person speaking. They are owning their views and feelings, which is always a true statement, not a controversial judgment.
  - o This communication approach can apply to more than two people, but the practice of it needs to be handled in pairs, not with everyone talking at the same time.

- This "Three Stools" approach does not apply well to conversations with people at your workplace; it is intended for committed relationships. Some people are fortunate to work with at least a few others who want to truly connect, in which case the communications approach here can be beneficial. However, work is intended in most cases to be a place where the directive style of the Thinking Stool dominates. Plans, opinions, judgments, and analysis that lead to directives are the mode of operation and the way projects are normally completed in a work environment. This book is about relationships, not business projects.

## About the "Three Stools" Approach

- This approach is new; but the underlying concepts have appeared in various forms in many other books and in couples workshops and retreats for decades. The intended difference here is the way it is presented. Hopefully, the explanations in this book are graphic through the use of the "Three Stools," each representing a separate part of who we are. Also, hopefully, the explanations are clear, easy to remember, and easy to practice with your partner … and practice, and practice.

- While the concepts here have been tested with couples and families and have been found to be easily understood, placing the concepts into practice proves to be more difficult. We are not automatically in touch with our inner-selves. Without conscious effort, we do not generally know what we are feeling or what we need emotionally, or how to speak to our partner about any of it, or how to listen to them if they try to convey to us what their inner world is at any given moment. We are most often focusing on the world outside ourselves; what we see and hear around us. We each have to learn to focus on our own internal world and how it changes with different situations. We each have to grow into being an introspective and responsive person. This book hopefully provides a good step in that direction.

- The "Three Stools" approach delineates how to express ourselves. The other side of a conversation, of course, is someone listening. Expression and listening must be integrated for the highest effectiveness overall. True listening will be summarized later in this chapter.

- Please try not to be discouraged if this learning is strange and difficult. Expect discomfort. Expect difficulty with understanding your own emotions and in speaking them. If you need a little help, see a counselor, a therapist, or a psychologist. Preferably find someone trained and experienced in couples and family therapy. A therapist with a degree in Marriage and Family Therapy (MFT) is the logical first choice for assisting with a relationship, but by talking to professionals in your geographic area, you may find others experienced in working with couples and families. I believe that virtually every couple or family who truly wants to do this work can.

## The Thinking Stool

 The first stool is that of Thinking, by which is meant analytical thinking. If you find yourself uncertain of the concept here, please review the Thinking Stool sections in Chapters 5 and 6.

  o This stool is the only one upon which arguments can occur. It is the only one where your partner or family member can claim you are wrong and they are right.

96

- Heated and disconnecting arguments occur as the couple sits, stands, and waves their arms from the tops of their respective Thinking Stools.
- Yet this stool is the place of work, economic progress, planning, and more. It is essential and valuable.
- In a relationship, this stool is often the source of each person feeling diminished and unheard: in other words, invalidated.
- The objective in a relationship is to always be honest, and the only way to do that while not invalidating your partner is to recognize your analytical thinking as your own. Your thoughts, opinions, judgments, et cetera are owned by you, not stated as if the world knows they are true and your partner is the only one who does not. You are being honest that you may be incorrect, but these are your thoughts and opinions: you "own" them. Your partner may have their thoughts, to which you will listen, but these are yours.
- In short, to continue to validate the other person in your relationship, be certain to *own* your opinions, thoughts, judgments, plans, explanations, solutions, and the like as yours. Stay honest in all ways by pointing out that you may be correct or incorrect, but these are your viewpoints. Finally, be open to *your partner's* thoughts, which they, too, must own.

## The Emotions Stool

 The next stool is that of Emotions. Of course, we all have emotions, but we are often unaware of the range of emotions coursing through us. Whether we notice them or not, emotions are a driving force in our lives. Emotions are the fuel and often the underlying motivation for our actions, our comments, and our behaviors. Again, to review these concepts, please read the earlier sections discussing the Emotions Stool. Remember that expressing our feelings …

- o Is a critical part of being able to know ourselves.
- o Is vital for our partner to understand us.
- o Allows others to understand our internal joys and our internal struggles.
- o Allows and helps create a connection between us and others on a truly personal and heartfelt level.
- o Allows our partner to better understand our behaviors, our actions, and our comments.
- o Helps our partner accept and believe in our willingness to be open and honest, which in turn creates more trust.
- o Reveals our internal world without attacking or diminishing our partner.
- o Allows perhaps the most important conversational connection that a couple can experience in a relationship.

## The Wants and Needs Stool

 The final stool is that of Wants and Needs— another aspect of ourselves that is often elusive. We need practice to learn to be aware of what we need and what we want. In 1943, Abraham

Maslow identified basic human needs in a hierarchy. The base or first level of the hierarchy is the need for physiological requirements such as food, shelter, and sleep. At this level, we are always aware of our needs. But as we travel up the hierarchy, we are less automatically aware; we have to force ourselves to pause to understand our own needs. Yet understanding our needs and being able to express them to our partner is vital for closeness in a relationship and for our own positive sense of Self. Maslow's work can be found in Chapter 5.

- Being able to connect with and express our Wants and Needs is important in relationships because ...

    o Expressing what we need or want at the moment is received very differently than angrily telling someone what to do.
    o Having unexpressed expectations rather than clarifying our needs can lead to our becoming unjustifiably angry.
    o The other person in the relationship—your partner, family member, or friend—can come to understand what is important to you rather than being unaware or confused.
    o We develop more of a sense of ourselves as we come to understand our own needs, wants, wishes, and dreams.
    o We come to understand more and more, as we speak up for ourselves, that we can and will be heard and accepted by our partner. They may not be able to provide our needs, wants, wishes and dreams, but they can hear them and accept our owning them.

# Listening More Slowly

- True listening requires energy; it is not a passive job. A listener who hears and seeks to understand exerts energy. The efforts and energies for true listening occur in two basic ways:

  o Focusing

  o Paraphrasing

- Focusing involves using one's energies to avoid distractions, to concentrate, and to internalize the words, thoughts, emotions, and expressed needs of the person talking.

- Paraphrasing has two components ...
  o One is repeating back the *content*: the actual story and information that your partner is attempting to make clear to you.
  o The second is conveying and honoring the underlying *emotions* of the person speaking. Your partner may not say they are frustrated, sad confused, or lonely, but your job as a true listener is to be a detective. Your job is to attempt to discern their underlying emotions, then inquire about those emotions and honor them.

- The value of saying back, or paraphrasing, to the other person your summary of what you heard is that it confirms for them that you received the message as they meant it. You validate them.

The next chapter provides example dialogues between couples, showing both the destructive conversations and the helpful, healthy "Three Stools" approach that uses the points above.

# Chapter 10
# Examples

*"Few things are harder to put up with than the annoyance of a good example."*

Mark Twain
(1835–1910), also
called Samuel
Clemens; American
humorist, lecturer,
writer, steamboat
captain, friend of
presidents and of
European royalty.

This chapter provides dialogues showing the differences between destructive, disconnecting arguments and the approaches described earlier in this book. The stories may seem familiar, but these stories and the people and pets in them are fictional.

The example dialogues will occur in two ways: first, the old destructive, argumentative way, and second, the new way. The new way will integrate the use of the "Three Stools" approach *and* the use of "Listening More Slowly."

## Example 1: Mary and John

Mary and John have a young border collie, Patches. He chases squirrels around their property and has never crossed the invisible electric fence that gives him a slight shock from his collar if he tries. John worries when Mary chooses to not place the shock collar on Patches when letting him out for the final run of the

101

evening. Mary believes that because Patches has never crossed the line, John does not need to worry. For her, putting the collar on is just a bother at a time when she is tired and simply wants to get to bed.

## The Old Way

First we will experience below the ineffective, argumentative conversation that often causes John and Mary to shut down. It goes something like this:

| | |
|---|---|
| John, exasperated: | "Look, I have told you all month that he needs to have that collar on. That's why we bought that ... *that* fence!" |
| Mary, angry: | "Leave me alone. Patches has never run away and he won't. You're just being stupid." |
| John, out of control: | "Get back here, Patches!!! Come here, Patches!!! Move out of the way ... I'll put the collar on myself!!!" |

We know what happens next in this story. John and Mary shut down; they do not talk for the rest of the night. John sleeps on the couch and is both happy and sad to be away from Mary. In the morning they are civil to each other but not kind. They barely speak. Each goes to work. In the evening they talk, but both are still shut down emotionally. Both are saying to themselves, "Why are we angry and shut down over a dog collar?" But they cannot, at the moment, claw their way out of their anger and depression. They stay in their shells, unhappy, sad, and confused.

Before experiencing the story from the position of the "Three Stools," let's discuss the underlying emotions each person is feeling before and during the argument.

**Before the Argument**, while letting Patches out the door without the collar ...

Mary's emotions as she is letting Patches outside (she may not yet be aware of these emotions):

- *Tired* from a long day.
- A bit *annoyed* because she does not see the collar.
- A bit *nervous* because she knows that John will not like the situation of Patches going outside without the collar.
- *Frustrated* that she has to even think of putting the collar on since Patches never crosses the line.
- *Determined* to simply stand her ground and let the dog out without the collar that she is unable to find easily.

John's emotions as he notices the collar is not on Patches (he may not yet be aware of these emotions):

- *Fear* that Patches might, this time, run through the invisible electric fence and be lost or hurt.
- *Frustrated* at Mary, thinking that she does not care about something that is crucial to him.
- *Rejected* and *hurt* stemming from his reaction to Mary rejecting the use of the collar, which is important to him.
- The hurt shows itself as *anger*; which is the emotion that is very much in charge of him at this point.

This hurt-driven anger leads to John's opening attack: "Look, I have told you all month that he needs to have that collar on. That's why we bought that ... *that* fence!"

Now that the argument has begun, let's explore the emotions lying deep inside each person **During the Argument:**

Mary's emotions upon hearing John's opening comment (she may not yet be aware of these emotions):
- o *Fear* that this argument will grow to something off the charts.
- o *Unappreciated* for letting the dog out in the first place; she is trying to help, she believes.
- o *Hurt* because she thinks that John is calling her "stupid" without actually saying the word.
- o *Controlled,* in that she is not being permitted to use her own judgment; she thinks John is trying to tell her what to do.
- o *Defensive,* to protect her rights and her choice.
- o *Enraged,* which is stemming from the hurt and the feeling of being controlled.
- o *Invalidated,* stemming from all the emotions and viewpoints of the situation.

John's emotions upon hearing Mary's reply, "Leave me alone. Patches has never run away and he won't. You're just being stupid." (John may not yet be aware of these emotions):
- o *Ignored,* because regardless of his attacking tone and show of concern, Mary appears to still not care.
- o *Rejected,* stemming from Mary's rejecting something he cares about.
- o *Fear* that the argument will grow.

104

- *Hurt* that Mary does not seem to care.
- *Defensive,* in an attempt to quell his own fears.
- *Invalidated,* stemming from Mary's comment of calling him stupid, and from his feeling ignored and rejected.

Having discussed the nature of arguments in earlier chapters, we can now observe several important points about this argument between John and Mary:

- If they were to talk to someone about this argument, they would probably both say something like, "It was an argument over something meaningless! It was about the dog's collar! How could we have been so upset and not talked with each other all night and all the next day over the dog's collar?"

  - Answer: As discussed earlier, the hurt and anger that fueled this argument was *not* stemming from the dog's collar. A sense of invalidation fueled this argument. Feeling invalidated is a powerful force.

- Neither Mary nor John expressed their internal emotions, wants, needs, or personal thoughts to the other. Neither appears, at this point, to be in touch with their own inner Self, and, therefore, they are unable to express anything except angry commands and defensive statements.

105

o Their apparent inability to handle the dog collar issue probably reflects their inability to discuss virtually any issue in a sharing, productive manner. They may rely upon humor or avoidance to get through disagreements without arguing. Said another way, when either of them is feeling unheard and unappreciated during a heated disagreement, those feelings in turn generate anger that they may attempt to cover with laugher, diversions, or avoidance. If asked, they would probably both say that they are carrying some significant level of anger with them nearly all of the time.

o This tension over the dog collar has existed between Mary and John for many months— perhaps even a year or two. It remains unsettled like an open wound. Further, this couple probably has several such open wounds. They may manage to be kind to each other; and even enjoy each other's company from time to time, but the relationship can be better. A heated, name-calling argument is not a sign of the healthiest possible relationship. If they make an effort to understand and apply the "Three Stools" approach, the relationship can grow to one of nearly constant emotional closeness, caring, and mutual understanding.

# The New Way

Let's now experience the new Mary and John. If we are imaginative here, we might say that the couple has returned from a retreat in which each became much more aware of their inner Self. Or perhaps they have read an informative article or book, talked, tried new behaviors, practiced, and arrived at this new state of trust and open vulnerability. Or perhaps they are working with a therapist. Whatever the path, here are the new Mary and John.

The situation is the same. Mary has chosen to let Patches into the yard without his shock collar. Remember from the above discussion that Mary had several emotions floating around as she made this decision.

Two basic versions of this dialogue exist for the new Mary and John. In one, Mary begins the dialogue, explaining her thoughts and concerns. In the other, Mary says nothing as she opens the door to let Patches out, so John has to begin the dialogue. In both versions, the couple will be practicing both the "Three Stools" approach and "Listening More Slowly." Words from the "Three Stools" approach are in italics.

## Version 1: Mary speaks first, as she begins to open the door for Patches ...

Mary: Standing near the back door with Patches next to her, she looks at John and says, "John, *I know* the collar is important to you, and I do *not want* to ignore that, but I am *tired*. Plus, I am *frustrated* that I can't find it."

107

| John: | Walking toward Mary while scanning for the collar, he chooses to begin by repeating back her comment, saying, "I hear you. You *don't want* to ignore *my wishes* to put the collar on, but you are *tired*." He then continues with his inner Self, saying, "I *know* what you mean, I am *exhausted*, too. Thanks for thinking of the collar. Maybe I can find it around here." |
|---|---|

Note that everything that Mary and John have said is absolutely true for each of them. They are simply speaking their own inner truths for each other to hear and understand. So far, this is effective. John feels like his spouse cares about him. Mary has vented her frustration while expressing her caring. Let's continue this dialogue a bit further.

| Mary: | "I would *like* to just forget the collar. We can't find it. I'm *tired and I'm frustrated*." |
|---|---|

| John: | Choosing again to show that he heard what she said, and to show that he cares, John begins with "I'm sorry you are *frustrated*." He then expresses his situation, saying, "Me too! Well … I *wish* I could let Patches outside without the collar, but I have this *fear* that haunts me. You know… that fear he will run away and something will happen." |
|---|---|

| Mary: | Wanting John to know she heard him, Mary paraphrases by saying, "I hear you, John. You are *afraid* Patches will run away. I *understand*." |
|---|---|

108

John: "Silly, I know! But I own this silly *fear*... it *feels real* to me."

Mary: "OK. So, I *need* to go to bed. I can't stand up. And tomorrow I *want* to find the collar. Meanwhile, this is *my opinion*: Here is the leash. Just wrap it around his neck and take him out for a walk in the yard. OK, sweetie?

John: "OK. Sounds good. Thanks. I *appreciate* your help. And I *need* to buy a spare collar this weekend!"

Please notice here that this couple is connected! Their joint frustration over the collar has actually brought them together! They are probably proud and delighted that they can work together under stress, and that they can remain close.

**Version 2: John speaks first as he notices that Patches is about to go outside without his collar ...**

John: "Wait ... hold it! Are you letting him go without his collar?"

Mary: "Yes. I know you *want* it on, but I'm *tired!*"

John: "It really *scares* me to let him outside without that collar! I just can't do it ... I *need* to have the collar on him."

Mary: Mary hears John owning his fear and notices he is not attacking her. She wants to support him by letting him know she heard him and understands. She paraphrases by saying, "I hear you. You are *afraid* he will run away, and it probably seems very *real* to you, and you *need* to have the collar on him."

John:    Feeling his anxiety melt down and drain away, John takes in a deep breath, then lets it out. He says, "Right. Sorry. I feel a little *silly* about it, but that's how it is."

Mary:    "OK. I *support* you in it, but I *need* to go to bed and I don't see the collar, so if you can walk him out, I will be *glad* to look for the collar tomorrow."

John:    "Fine. No problem. Thanks for *understanding.* And this weekend I *hope* to buy a spare collar so you and I are not so *frustrated* about this. Goodnight, Pumpkin."

So, a couple can choose to have a shared, caring conversation in which they each express their own inner Self and through that find a solution, or to try to control the situation, which leads to each person feeling invalidated, angry, and frustrated, with little hope for a solution that creates closeness. The new Mary and John chose the former.

# Example 2: Kate and Andy

Kate and Andy pass each other on the stairs as Kate is leaving three-year-old Angela's room, having just read the child's favorite bedtime story and watched her become sleepy ... finally. Andy is on his way up the stairs to spend time with Angela. He just arrived home from a long day and miles of traffic.

As they pass on the stairs, Kate is exhausted and highly nervous that Andy will wake Angela. We do not have to reenact the details of the old dialogue that might happen here. Basically, it might start with Kate asking Andy where he is going; he would reply that he is going to see Angela before she goes to sleep; Kate would complain that she just spent an hour getting Angela into bed; Andy would argue that he will just be a couple of minutes; and on it would go, with temperatures rising. It could be a bit nasty, with each person feeling unheard, and with anger at the end of a short yelling match that would wake up Angela.

Now let's eavesdrop on the new Kate and Andy way of communicating. Remember, personal and owned opinions, wants, needs, and feelings are in italics:

# The New Way

Kate:
As she passes Andy bounding up the stairs:
"Hey, there! Hello! I *feel better* just seeing you! I was a bit *worried*. It is nearly 8:00. How are you?" She gives Andy a hug on the stairs.

Andy:
Hugging back, he says:
"I am *exhausted*. I *miss* you and my little girl. I *want* to see her. It has been all day."

111

Kate:            "Well, I hear you … you are *exhausted*, and you *miss* seeing Angela, and you are *eager* to see her. Right?" Andy agrees. Her paraphrasing was correct. Kate continues, "Oh, Andy, I am so *worried* she will *not want* to get back in bed. I am *exhausted* with putting her to sleep. It took me an hour. And now it is way past her bedtime. I am *worried* about how she will be tomorrow."

At this point in this introspective and interpersonal conversation, the solution between Kate and Andy could be …

   o That Andy recognizes and expresses his shared concern about Angela's sleep, and, in addition, he wants to honor Kate's worry. He offers a solution of seeing Angela in the morning, or of leaving her a drawing and a note that Mom will read to her. He decides, in other words, to not wake Angela.

Or the solution could be …

   o That Andy expresses his strong need to see and hug Angela. In turn, Kate recognizes that desire and need of Andy's and agrees to support Andy in going to Angela, but she might place some limits, such as that Andy cannot let her get out of bed, or he cannot read her a long story.

Again, the old way leads to anger and no shared resolution. Not only would the couple be upset, but their child, Angela, might well hear the argument and the anger and become upset herself. The new way provides connection, sharing, caring, and a wonderful environment for everyone, including their child.

Can you feel the difference in the old way and the new way in these examples? Without the new way of expressing and listening, the hurt and anger is thick. Each person is shut down, becomes isolated, and is virtually unable to feel open to their partner. Some level of hopelessness and sadness begins to mix with the anger and hurt.

The new way of communicating by expressing and by listening creates closeness. It may not be perfect, in that some level of frustration may still be present, but overall couples can become connected. Life shows more love, meaning, and purpose.

Occasionally, during counseling sessions, someone will express to me their doubt that "such a subtle difference in the way we talk to each other will matter." Yet the difference is not subtle. In fact, it is difficult to do what appears to be simple, namely, "To thine own self be true" (Chapter 6).

> To express one's own emotions is much more difficult than people first realize, but closeness in relationships is the reward for the effort.

In this life we cannot do great things.
We can only do small things with great
love.

Mother Teresa

# Chapter 11
# Your Turn

New discussions like the ones above are the glue of wonderful relationships. *Difficult situations are opportunities* for two people who care about each other and about sharing to come together to discuss problems by expressing their inner Selves to each other. Each person can thereby feel included, validated, and acknowledged for who they are. You have met the new Mary and John and the new Kate and Andy. Now it is your turn.

Thanks for reading this short book. I wish you and yours all the best as you travel this journey. Please remember that finding a professional to assist you is often a wise step along this journey. People are often a bit fearful to ask for professional help because they are uncertain of what they will experience. Remember, please, that the sessions are yours. You can gain from them what you need and what you seek. Feel your fear, but grow through it.

If the fear is strong, then think about beginning by wading into the experience of speaking from within yourself. Rather than diving in, which can certainly feel scary, think of taking small steps. See what you and your partner experience, then take the next step when you are ready. Finally, please read, or at least scan, the Appendix sections:

- o   His and Her Brain
- o   Feeling Words
- o   Selected Readings

All the best,
Bill Montgomery

There are other beaches to explore.
There are more shells to find.
This is only the beginning.

Anne Morrow Lindbergh
from her book,
"Gift from the Sea"

# Appendix 1
# His and Her Brain

This Appendix provides a brief overview of the basic development and the structural layout of the female and male human brain as a way to help explain differences in the perceptions and innate communications styles of women and men. Remember, however, that we can all modify and improve our styles of communicating through learning various skills, including those in Chapters 1 through 10 of this book. We need not feel stuck because of our genes and chromosomes. Female and male brains, and therefore behaviors, have innate differences, but we can all learn and all improve. Couples can feel and be closer.

Findings about the differences between male and female brains are fascinating. Much of the behavior of children, teenagers, dating couples, longtime couples, and new fathers and mothers can be explained by central nervous system makeup and how it changes both over time and with impactful situations. But let's be careful here. Organic, gender-determined differences do not and cannot explain everything. Most importantly, we are all individuals. Not only is each person's organic internal makeup different from everyone else's, but the childhood experiences that help form each of us are different. Even twins raised in the same household experience their childhoods differently, so they are affected differently. Part of who we are comes from the organic side, our genes. The other part comes from our experiences as we grow. Our genetic makeup is unique for all of us, and our specific childhood experiences are unique for all of us. We are all different, therefore, not only in physical appearance, but in personality. Further, and most importantly for the purposes of this book, we can learn to change. We can improve our relationships and our experience in life by learning a few basic skills about communicating with others, especially with our partners ... those people who are here to support us and to be loving listeners. In short, while our genes and our childhood have formed us, the forming is not over. We can learn new skills that help add joy and connection to our lives.

We all recognize basic differences between the interests and the behaviors of males and females. For example, a desire to talk about feelings, caring about how a friend is handling an emotional situation, some but not generally high interest in competition, and joy in holding an infant are most often female traits. Male traits would be, in general and not always, the opposite of these. So, we know there are basic differences to be expected.

A variety of studies over many years has concluded that women and men have the same average intelligence: that is, IQ levels are statistically the same. Differences do exist in average female and male scores on certain areas of an IQ test, but the overall averages are the same. For example, women tend to score higher on certain verbal and memory tests, whereas men tend to score higher on mathematical and spatial tests, particularly mental spatial rotations. These differences can be largely explained by differences in the makeup of women's brains compared to men's, but the main point is that overall, intelligence is the same. Furthermore, regardless of gender, we have the same capability to do various jobs and hobbies, from crafts and construction to surgery and pharmacy to being ministers, politicians, managers, clerks, pilots, gardeners, financial planners, and engineers. While tendencies exist for certain genders to follow certain professions, no gender-related brain or hormonal differences prevent us from being anything we wish.

# Same but Different

While women and men have the same overall average level of intelligence and are mentally capable of the same jobs, careers, vocations and avocations, there is a difference in academic interests shown by females versus males. While some of the difference may be related to classroom settings that are comfortable for girls compared to what is comfortable for boys, neuropsychiatrists suggest something else. In particular, during the teenage years, girls show less interest in math and science than boys primarily because their central nervous systems are experiencing an influx of typical female hormones—estrogen and oxytocin—that stimulate them to seek connection with others, to chat, to develop friendships, and to concentrate on their appearance. The teen years are not the best time for most young girls to be exploring their interest in the sciences, researchers find.

All of this in no way means that young girls are incapable of certain studies: of course not. But it does mean that for most young girls there is a tendency to lean toward social connection, including academic studies that are more socially oriented, rather than toward impersonal subjects. Contrarily, a strong interest in math or science, or a strong interest in achieving a career in medicine, or as a math teacher, researcher, or the like, can overpower the hormonal push toward social connection and stimulate the young girl to succeed in achieving her own personal dreams. The general tendency for teen girls, however, is toward social connection.

Teenage boys, being flooded with the male hormones testosterone and vasopressin, are more interested in their individual work and in competition. Classes in subjects stressing facts, theory, spatial relation, or logical thinking, such as math and science, wood or metal shop, and even sports are compatible with their focusing tendencies at this time in their life. Again, interest in art, music, social studies, history, and other social-concept-related areas can certainly overcome hormonal pushes toward being primarily individualistic. We all recognize that many young boys can be socially oriented and can seek careers involving social connection. The general tendency, however, is for individualism. Even if an adolescent male seeks social events like parties, or to be part of a football team or part of the science club, we can expect to find competition and a striving toward recognition for individual effort.

## Let's Talk Chemistry

The word "hormone" is defined in most dictionaries as "a chemical messenger that carries a signal from one part of the body to another via the bloodstream." In other words, muscles and bones grow, skin remains flexible, blood pressure stabilizes, sexual interest peaks, blood sugar decreases, and kidneys function all under the influence of hormones sending signals from one part of the body to another. Usually the path is between some specific part of the brain and a particular organ, like the kidneys or the heart. Estrogen, oxytocin, testosterone, vasopressin, and cortisol are only five of the many hormones running through the most amazing machines in the world: our bodies.

Neurochemicals are a special class of hormones that are created in, and essentially stay within, the nerve tissue; the prefix "neuro" means "nerves." Mood-creating neurochemicals, for example, are made by various sections of the brain and released into other sections. Further, acceptance of these neurochemicals by a selected section of the brain requires the presence of receptors that can absorb them. An analogy would be that a football is meant to pass through goal posts and a basketball is meant for a hoop; mixing them is unacceptable. Our moods, including feelings of joy, love, anger, depression, sadness, loneliness, and anxiety, are all highly dependent upon the levels and the mix of our neurochemicals and upon the number of receptors available to be activated. If receptors are not available or are overly available due to stress or some genetic tendency, mood may be affected differently than if the receptor count were more normal.

Serotonin, dopamine, and norepinephrine are the three most common neurochemicals. More specifically, these three are called neurotransmitters because they transmit themselves from a nerve transmitter ending to a receptor ending. Further, very small amounts of these chemicals are required: on the order of fractions of a drop in the brain. Too little leads to depression and perhaps worse; too much leads to anxiety and perhaps worse. As you have probably guessed by now, antidepressants work to essentially increase these three brain chemicals. Also, alcohol acts in ways that temporarily increases some of these neurochemicals, which explains the temporary feelings of energy and extraversion we experience before the depressant effects of alcohol set in, causing calm, sleep, and sometimes depression. Long-term use of alcohol at significant levels typically amplifies depression over time.

Interestingly, females and males have virtually the same hormones and neurochemicals, but in different levels. And these different chemical levels, although they involve very small amounts, create a large difference in thinking, emotions, and behavior. Further, these levels fluctuate day-to-day; the degree of fluctuation depends upon whether the person is male or female, their age, and their eating, drinking, and exercise habits. Be assured, our chemical brain-mix is on the move; moody days are real. Joyful, ebullient days can likewise be the result of hormonal changes, which may be short or long-lasting, depending on the circumstances that triggered the change.

The difference in the chemical mix for women and men begins before childhood; even before birth. The male hormone testosterone is released within the embryo after about eight weeks in the uterus. In contrast, estrogen begins to be released in the young girl at about one month after birth. The effects of these and related hormones on the behavior and interests of male and female infants are noticeable and continue to affect development for decades. Yet teenagers and mature adults have both testosterone and estrogen, regardless of gender; again, the mix makes the difference. Further, men and women have a range of hormones and neurochemicals depending upon the person. Some women are low in what we think of as women's chemistry, and some are high. Some men are low in men's chemistry; some are high. Nothing about us is a fixed template. We are all different.

## Let's Talk Brain Architecture

Brain structure and brain chemistry differences begin before we are born and continue into our elder years. The microscopic structures of the male and female brain are indeed different, and that difference begins with the embryo's acknowledgement of a male XY chromosome pair versus a female's XX pairing. The female brain structure appears to promote more relationship with others: more connection, more emotional understanding of herself and of others. Studies show that week-old female infants are better at reading faces and noticing emotional tones in voices than are male infants. The mature female brain promotes motherhood, nurturing, emotional protection of the family, and a desire for social harmony. The male brain structure from a young age promotes competition, individual effort, physical protection of the family, and a bent toward leading and guiding the family.

Certain architectures are known to be different. Male sex drive, for example, is associated with a brain area called the "area of sexual pursuit," an area that is at least twice as large in males compared to females. Conversely, females have a larger hippocampus area, which relates to the female's stronger interest in relationships and to better memory about romantic moments and disturbing fights. Different interests and different abilities are accounted for by such structural differences, and also by our environments as our brains developed, especially during our formative years. Further, different environments can affect how our brain processes and develops, and thereby can affect our intellectual interests; our emotional makeup, including our ability to regulate our emotions; and our spiritual leanings.

Knowing these basic differences can provide each of us with insight and better understanding about who we are: our natural tendencies and our natural strengths and weaknesses. Remember, however, that we are all capable of altering those tendencies or weaknesses that may interfere with developing the types of relationships we deeply want with our partners. No two brains in the world are identical, no two childhood experiences are identical, and no two people are identical. As a result, no two people have the same exact interests, attitudes, emotional responses, spiritual leanings, or intelligence at the same level in the same areas. While we are all different, we are nonetheless capable of modifying those parts of our intellect and emotions that will allow us to connect better with others, especially our partners.

## Old Brain, New Tricks

"Old dogs can't learn new tricks" is generally not true for dogs, or for humans. The mental and emotional parts of us can learn new ways to interact and to enjoy relationships. Decades ago, most social and behavioral researchers theorized that by adolescence and young adulthood, personality had been formed, the person was well defined, and changes after that would be subtle and modest.

Today we understand more. We understand that brain structure and chemistry continue to change over time, with continued growth of synaptic connections well into our thirties, and with other adjustments automatically occurring throughout our lives. Our brain structures and neurochemical mixes change throughout our lives. Have you ever noticed that as a person ages into their 70s and 80s, their ears grow larger? Clearly the body is at work, growing in different ways even when it is older. So, how can we possibly be surprised that our brain systems are also changing and adapting for our entire lives? Further, we understand today that as people work on their emotional issues, perhaps especially the issues within their relationships, they are able to change their underlying assumptions, beliefs, trust levels, and behaviors. Contentious relationships can become whole again.

The changes that people can experience in levels of trust and comfort come with changes in their brain structures and neurochemistry. In other words, as you and/or your partner work to see the relationship differently, you will be changing what happens in your brain. It is as if your ears grow bigger as you work on the relationship. Learning and practicing the "Three Stools" approach to communications in this book will change how your brain functions. The change may be so small that it cannot be seen on a brain scan or MRI, but small changes can have enormous effects on you and your relationships.

If you are wondering about simply taking antidepressants to effect the changes, you may be partially correct. Antidepressants can help take the edge off of anxiety and depression. While antidepressants do not grow areas in the brain relating to trust, help a person learn empathy, or help them learn how to express their pain to a loving listener, medication can lower anxiety and depression sufficiently to allow more openness and willingness to communicate with new skills. These skills and these ways of becoming open and even vulnerable are learnable and will change relationships and levels of happiness and comfort. In other words, we are in charge of what we learn and practice, and as we learn, our brains change. Our hearts can grow fonder.

# Appendix 2
# Feeling Words

## Imagine saying, "I feel ..."

abandoned, abashed, able-bodied, absent, absent-minded, aghast, abrupt, absolved.

absorbed, abused, accepted, accountable, active, adaptable, addicted, admired, adored, affectionate, afraid, aggravated, aggressive, agitated, alarmed, alert, alienated, alive, alone, aloof, alluring, amazed, ambushed, amused, angry, antagonistic, annoyed, anxious, apathetic, appalled, apologetic, appreciated, appreciative, apprehensive, approachable, aroused, ashamed, assertive, astonished, attacked, attractive, aware, awful, awkward

bad, baffled, bashful, beaten-down, beat-up, belittled, benevolent, berated, betrayed, bewildered, bitter, blamed, blue, bold, bored, bossed, bossy, bothered, brave, broken, bummed-out, burdened, burned-out

calm, candid, capable, carefree, careful, careless, caring, cautious, centered, certain, challenged, charmed, cheated, cheerful, cherished, childish, clean, clear, clever, close,

closed, clueless, clumsy, cold, comfortable, committed, compassionate, competent, competitive, complacent, complete, concerned, condemned, confident, confused, considerate, content, controlled, convicted, courageous, cowardly, cranky, crazy, cross, crushed, curious

daring, dazed, dead, deceived, dedicated, defeated, defenseless, defensive, defiant, degraded, dejected, delicate, delighted, demoralized, dependent, depressed, deprived, deserted, desired, despair, desperate, destroyed, detached, determined, devastated, devious, devoted, different, difficult, dirty, disappointed, disbelieving, discarded, disconnected, discontent, discouraged, disgraced, disgusted, disheartened, dishonest, disillusioned, dismal, dismayed, disobedient, disorganized, disposable, distant, distracted, distressed, disturbed, doubtful, drained, dread, dull, dumb

127

eager, ecstatic, edgy, effective, embarrassed, empathetic, empty, enchanted, encouraged, energetic, energized, elated, enlightened, enraged, enriched, entertained, enthusiastic, envious, equal, evasive, evil, exasperated, excited, excluded, exhausted, exhilarated, exploited, exposed, exuberant

faithful, fake, fantastic, fatigued, fearful, fearless, feisty, fine, flustered, foolish, forgiven, forgiving, forgotten, fortunate, framed, frantic, free, friendly, frightened, frisky, frustrated, fulfilled, full, funny, furious

generous, gentle, giving, grieving, glorious, good, grateful, great, glad, gloomy, grouchy, guarded, guilty, gullible

happy, hateful, haunted, healthy, heard, heartbroken, helpful, helpless, hesitant, honored, hopeful, hopeless, horrible, horrified, horrific, hospitable, hostile, humble, humiliated, hurt, hysterical

idealistic, idiotic, ignorant, ignored, imaginative, immune, impatient, imperfect, impertinent, important, impressed, impulsive, inadequate, inattentive, incensed, incompetent, incomplete, incredulous,

indebted, indecisive, independent, indifferent, industrious, inept, inferior, inflated, informed, infuriated, inhibited, innocent, innovative, inquisitive, insane, insecure, insensitive, insignificant, isolated, insulted, intense, interested, interrogated, interrupted, intimidated, intimate, intrigued, invalidated, invigorated, invisible, involved, irrational, irresponsible, irritated

jazzy, jealous, jinxed, jolly, jovial, joyful, jubilant, judged, judgmental, jumpy, just, justified

kicked, kidded, kind, knowledgeable

late, lazy, leery, left out, let down, liable, liberated, lifeless, lighthearted, liked, logical, lonely, loose, lost, lousy, lovable, loved, loving, lucky

mad, manipulated, mean, meditative, melancholy, merry, mischievous, miserable, misinterpreted, mistreated, misunderstood, mixed up, mocked, modest, molested, moody, motivated, moved, mystified

naïve, nasty, needed, needy, negative, neglected, nervous, neurotic, nostalgic, noticed, numb obeyed, obligated, obvious, odd, offended, old, open, oppressed, optimistic, ornery, out of control, outraged, overcome, overjoyed, overloaded, overwhelmed, overworked, owned

pampered, paralyzed, passionate, passive, patient, peaceful, peeved, pensive, perky, perplexed, persecuted, pessimistic, pestered, petrified, petty, phony, pious, playful, pleased, poor, possessive, positive, powerful, powerless, practical, pressured, private, productive, protected, protective, proud, provoked, prudish, punished, pushy, puzzled

questioned, quiet

reassured, realistic, rebellious, reborn, receptive, reckless, recognized, reconciled, refreshed, regretful, rejected, rejuvenated, relaxed, released, relieved, reluctant, remorseful, renewed, replaced, replenished, repressed, rescued, resentful, reserved, resistant, resourceful, respected, responsible, restricted, revengeful, revitalized, rich, ridiculous, right, rigid, robbed, romantic, rotten, rushed

sabotaged, sad, safe, sassy, satisfied, saved, scared, scolded, scorned, secure,

seductive, self-assured, self-centered, self-confident, self-conscious, self-destructive, self-reliant, selfish, sensitive, sentimental, serene, serious, sexy, skillful, shamed, shaken, sheepish, shocked, shunned, shy, sick, silenced, silly, sincere, sinful, slandered, sluggish, small, smart, smothered, skeptical, solemn, soothed, sorry, special, spiteful, splendid, spunky, squashed, stifled, stimulated, stingy, strained, stretched, stressed, strong, stubborn, stumped, stunned, stupid, submissive, successful, suicidal, suffocated, sullen, sunk, super, superior, supported, sure, surly, surprised, suspicious, sympathetic

tacky, tactful, talented, talkative, tame, tarnished, tasteful, tearful, teased, tenacious, tender, tense, terrible, terrific, terrified, tested, thankful, thoughtful, threatened, thrifty, thrilled, tired, tormented, tortured, tough, tragic, transformed, trapped, treasured, tremendous, tricked, troubled, trusted

ugly, unaccepted, unappreciated, unbalanced, unburdened, uncomfortable, unconcerned, unfit, unfriendly, united, unknown, unneeded, unpleasant, unreal, unruly, unwise, uplifted, used, useless

vacant, vague, vain, validated,
valued, vicious, victimized,
victorious, violated, vivid,
voided

warm, warmhearted, warned,
wary, wasted, weak, wealthy,
weary, weird, whole, wild,
willful, wishful, witty, worldly,
worthy, wounded, wronged

yielding, young, youthful

# Appendix 3
# Selected Readings

The following books have been widely recognized as informative for a better understanding of relationships and for ways to improve those relationships. They are written for the general public, not specifically for therapists. Several of these have been used as general references in writing this book.

## 1. Marriage and Partnerships

*The Angry Marriage: Overcoming the Rage, Reclaiming the Love*, by Bonnie Maslin, Ph.D.
> Describes various types of angry marital "styles," how to recognize them, and how to work through them. Many examples are used throughout the book.

*We Can Work It Out: How to Solve Conflicts, Save Your Marriage, and Strengthen Your Love for Each Other*, by Clifford Notarius, Ph.D. and Howard Markman, Ph.D.
> With an emphasis on better ways to communicate, this book addresses ways to approach reducing and resolving arguments.

*Keeping the Love You Find*, by Harville Hendix, Ph.D.
> This psychology-oriented book introduces the term "Imago," which is Latin for image, as a way of explaining the influence that our parents, early teachers, and other caretakers have on our unconscious and therefore on the partners we choose as adults. The book also addresses other personality factors and suggests ways to improve relationships.

*Why Marriages Succeed or Fail, and How You Can Make Yours Last*, by John Gottman, Ph.D.

The author has studied marriage issues for over 20 years in a near-laboratory setting in order to evaluate ways to improve the marriage relationship. The book contains basic findings and offers exercises, quizzes, and tips that are intended to strengthen marriages.

*The 7 Stages of Marriage*, by Rita DeMaria, Ph.D. and Sari Harrar.

The authors identify seven stages of marriage, starting with "Passion," and offer techniques for "feeling happy and secure" in each stage. The book is written in an upbeat, friendly style with exercises, tips, guidance, and an easy-to-follow structure.

## 2. Our Inner Child Affects Relationships
*Homecoming: Reclaiming and Championing Your Inner Child*, by John Bradshaw.

First made popular by his PBS television series on Family Healing, Bradshaw explores the inner child in all of us along with the needs and fears of that child. By creating awareness and through various exercises in the book, the inner child can be calmed and relationships can improve.

## 3. Our Central Nervous System Affects Relationships
*The Female Brain*, by Louann Brizendine, M.D.

The book describes the development of the female brain, and to some extent the male brain, from birth through teen years to courting, pregnancy, childbirth, and beyond, pointing out how each event creates a change. A book on the male brain is forthcoming.

*Synaptic Self*, by Joseph LeDoux, Ph.D.

A synapse is a space between brain cells, and the vast network of synapses produces our thinking, our five senses, and our emotions. This book provides the general reader with a scientific discussion of how our brains work and the effect on relationships.

## 4. Parenting

*Parenting from the Inside Out: How a Deeper Self-Understanding Can Help You Raise Children Who Thrive*, by Daniel Siegel, M.D. and Mary Hartzell, M. Ed.

The authors offer parents an approach to forming a deeper understanding of their own life stories that will, in turn, help them raise compassionate, resilient, and family-connected children. The book is unique in its approach to educating parents about the effects of relationships on their own development from a neurological and emotional viewpoint, in order to better enable improved connection with their children.

*How to Get Your Teen to Talk to You*, by Connie Grigsby and Kent Julian.

If you are the parent or loving caregiver of a teenager, research consistently shows that you are the most important person in their life, even if they do not act as if that is true. This book on how to communicate with your teen gives tips and tools that can help improve your relationship with your teen.

*You're Wearing That?—Understanding Mothers and Daughters in Conversation*, by Deborah Tannen.

Tannen writes on the back cover of her book, "Mothers and daughters speak the same language—but often misunderstand each other as they struggle to find the balance between closeness and independence." Tannen explores the reasons and explains new approaches

Everything that lives, lives not alone, nor for itself.

William Blake, 1757–1827, English poet and painter, largely unknown during his lifetime, but now considered by some to be "the greatest artist Britain ever produced."

# The Author

William L. Montgomery
(Photo on back cover)

Bill is a practicing therapist and counselor in Doylestown, PA, with the Council for Relationships and with Lenape Valley Foundation. Bill has received recognition for his work with adults, couples, teenagers, children, and families. He helps people find their way out of depression, anger, couples' stress, marital discourse, parental difficulties, mistrust, addiction, trauma, loss, harmful behavior, attention issues, and more.

Before Doylestown, Bill worked in corporations, was an independent consultant, and was dean of the National Graduate School in Falmouth, MA. He has completed three master's degrees and a Ph.D. in various areas, including a master's degree in Marriage and Family Therapy. He is also a certified Gestalt Therapist; a training that shows how to use interesting and insightful approaches to understanding one's self.

Bill and his wife Loretta, who is an abstract artist, a hospital volunteer, and more, have four adult daughters and two grandchildren, all of whom add special relationships and extra dimensions to their lives.

Contact:
215-489-0826

# The Editor

Tahlia Day

Tahlia is known as an exacting yet creative proofreader and editor who has additional talent as an interpretative and abstract artist. Living near Madison, Wisconsin, she studied at Bryn Mawr College and the School of the Art Institute of Chicago. In her art, Tahlia works primarily in watercolor, ink, and mixed media. You can see her work and more information at tahliaday.com or katharosediting.com.

# The Illustrator

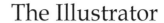

Bonnie Long

A lifelong artist, Bonnie Long, now of Princeton, NJ, formerly of Yardley, PA, works in a variety of media: watercolor, oil, acrylic, pencil, pastel, stone, and wire sculpture. Reading and traveling pique her curiosity and her self-admitted quirkiness. She has studied at the Pennsylvania Academy of Art, and has won a variety of awards in and around Philadelphia. Bonnie and her work are much admired, as is her participation in a number of art and garden groups, from the New Hope Art League to the American Botanical Artists Society.

Bonnie and her significant other, George Taylor, who has a company that develops and commercially installs large devices for generating electricity from ocean waves, have an extended group of family and friends that adds to the variety of their travels and their interests.

"Come," he added, "try it and see!"

"The Adventures of Pinocchio"
by Carlo Collodi, 1883